THE WONDER OF TOUCH

THE WONDER OF TOUCH

William E. Dorman

RESOURCE *Publications* • Eugene, Oregon

THE WONDER OF TOUCH

Resource Publications
An Imprint of Wipf and Stock Publishers
199 W. 8th Ave., Suite 3
Eugene, OR 97401

www.wipfandstock.com

PAPERBACK ISBN: 978-1-7252-9300-7
HARDCOVER ISBN: 978-1-7252-9299-4
EBOOK ISBN: 978-1-7252-9301-4

04/15/21

To Mary Frances Gardner Dorman, my editor-in-chief, and soulmate. Her insights kept this book afloat, and on course.

CONTENTS

FOREWORD

Touch is one of our five senses. It is a physical reality. Touch is a capacity of our fingers, and extends throughout and across our largest organ—our skin. Given our opposing thumb, we can grip, doing so with a firm hold, or a gentle clasp. Touch sends us warning signals of the dangers in sharp edges, and hot surfaces. Through caresses, we express tenderness, and exchange loving messages. Conversely, touch is tragically the malevolent means of aggression, dominance, abuse, and violence.

Touch is more than tactile. It is spiritual. Touch is a sense essential to the human longing to belong. At the spiritual and emotional levels, being in touch is how we experience that we are united within ourselves. Spiritual and emotional touch is the path to being one, to communing with ourselves, others, creation, and the Greatest Mystery. I explore and discuss both tactile and spiritual touch in the following chapters.

The upsurge of loneliness in our society is one signal that we hunger for spiritual and emotional touch (*Born to Be Good: The Science of a Meaningful Life*, Norton, 2009.) We are losing touch with our deepest self, and losing touch with those who matter most to us. Rage, war, and prejudice raise red welts on society's skin, signs that we have lost touch with our neighbors, near and far. With the loss of touch, incidents of depression continue to increase, revealing the loss of touch with meaning and purpose. The prevalence of myriad addictions trumpets how we have lost touch with relationships and interactions, secluding ourselves in a variety of isolating substances or electronic cocoons.

The pain of emptiness points to the lost touch with the Greatest Mystery, the source of Boundless Love. Absent this touch, people feel unimportant, and unloved. The remedy for this emptiness is the experience of being touched by the Greatest Mystery. This touch is the message of hope and healing that our planet awaits.

The earth itself is loudly proclaiming that we are out of touch with nature—its life-forms, soil, atmosphere, bodies of water. Earth displays the grief and anguish it is experiencing at the loss of human touch and care. The hurricanes, forest fires, rising sea levels, polluted water, foul air, and massive rainfall and flooding all signal how earth is dis-eased.

PREFACE

This book is written for those who know the apprehension and pain of being out of touch. Even a casual observer knows that in this nation particularly, many people have lost touch with the Holy, the Other, the deepest self, and Mother Earth. We dwell in existentially and spiritually distressing times.

There is a balm for these maladies. This balm is a healing touch, one that conveys to people that they matter, are unconditionally loved, and that they are a part of a larger whole. This awareness is the wonder of touch as it affects our body, mind, and spirit. This book is about that healing touch experienced in relationship with the Greatest Mystery.

Acknowledgments

This book is a community event. My family, and circle of friends, have been sources of encouragement and support in the writing of this book. I thank Rabbi Paul Citrin, a dear friend and colleague, for his thorough reading of the manuscript, and for providing me an invaluable critique, helpful suggestions, and productive comments. Fran, my in-house editor-in-chief, and main collaborator, was unfailing in reading and rereading the manuscript in its many stages and iterations. She kindly, and firmly, guided me in writing, and rewriting in order to improve the book.

INTRODUCTION

For a book begun in 2018, it arrives at just the opportune time. Lacking foreknowledge of the coronavirus, and the human toll it would, and is exacting, the book draws attention to the despair and despondency caused by the absence of touch. It upholds as well the hope and healing touch grants us, and all creation.

Prior to COVID-19, we took touch for granted. We greeted one another with handshakes, hugs, pats on shoulder and back, and kisses. Our health care professionals—dentists, nurses, primary care physicians, nurse practitioners, physician's assistants, medical and nursing assistants—and others involved in addressing our health, all touched us.

We took socializing in its varied forms for granted. We gave no thought to attending movies, eating out, worshipping at church or synagogue or mosque, going to concerts, playing in the band, singing in the choir, traveling by whatever means to wherever we wanted to visit, going to our child's or professional sporting events to cheer for our team, throwing parties and family gatherings in our homes, stopping at a friends' homes. Certainly, we went to weddings, funerals, anniversaries, and visited our family and friends who were hospitalized, or required assisted-living settings. It was a given that we were present at our loved ones' sick beds and death beds.

A book about touch is timely because today's absence of, and limits on, human touch are taking their toll. Levels of stress, depression, suicide, substance abuse, and addiction are at an all-time high, and climbing. The family home is now a workplace, schoolhouse, and residence. School- and university-age individuals lack the stimulation and nourishment of the community of learning, encouragement, support, and interaction that we call "school." Given the ebb and flow of the virus, regulations and restrictions as to who, how many, for what reason, and where people may gather fluctuates.

The dearth of touch presently available offers a sparse diet. It is this radical unavailability of touch that is excruciatingly painful. The "touch desert" we now tread highlights the life-giving importance of touch—touch both tangible and intangible.

My book discusses and describes the experience of touch in this dual perspective. A hug, such a common frequent experience, is an example of this double valence of touch. A hug is nourishing, a physical and literal touch, which is felt externally on shoulders, arms, and back. The hug simultaneously touches the heart, soul, and mind of the one receiving the hug in an intangible and metaphorical manner, and of the one giving the hug.

Creation is saddened by how we take it for granted, how we abuse it. Nature writhes in pain from our blows. Its anger is witnessed by the rising temperature of the atmosphere and the oceans. Creation pleads with us to love it, sending us messages with the furious storms, the melting ice fields, the rising oceans. That message is: "Restore your love for me, and I will love and bless you in return."

COVID-19 is not the sole cause for the absence of touch. The principalities and powers of self-centeredness and "me first" are fragmenting and dividing our nation. Touch is difficult, if not improbable, under such circumstances. Selfishness puts us out of touch with the Transcendent in creation. The spiritual emptiness we witness underscores the yearning to touch, and be touched by, the Sacred Spirit.

Touch's power to heal hearts, minds, souls, communities, and creation is the crux of this book. We live in a biosphere of touch where we flourish when our interrelatedness is robust and healthy.

For the sake of Mother Earth, and the continuance of the human species, now is the time to renew and restore being in touch.

WHERE WE ARE TODAY

The world that we see in the not-too-distant-future is bleak. As a matter of fact, to a great many, the present itself is dreary, and dismal. We are not a people who await a Utopia, a return of the garden of Eden, or a grand Golden Age. No, we foresee a Dystopia: cities in rubble; governments that are militaristic, totalitarian, and dictatorial; an earth that is blighted and fighting for its very existence. The extinction of the human race is an ever-growing possibility.

In the face of this gloom, humans remain resilient. While we possess such a dismal view of the future, we continue to hold onto hope. We yearn for hope, something that will lift our spirits, spur our imaginations, stir our thoughts, and move our hearts to perform deeds of love, and justice. We want this hope anchored in experience, something we can get our hands on, a hope that is tangible—a hope of substance.

The life-giving hope that we want, and need, is one that comes from touch. This touch is both tangible, and metaphorical. It involves hands, hands that reach out to touch other hands, and pat shoulders. It consists of caring words, gestures, and deeds touching human hearts and minds. This hope must be strong, as it faces formidable foes.

Is it any accident that our culture is awash with male and female superheroes, beings with matchless powers, and all but invulnerable? This array of superheroes is nothing but the personification of hope. With these heroes abounding, we mere mortals can look to the heavens for our salvation.

We can have hope that evil will not prevail, that injustice shall be called to account, that good shall triumph over wrong. No challenge is beyond their ability to confront and resolve positively. Our hearts swell with hope as we witness their victorious and just exploits.

This book brings hope, hope as living water for those who thirst for hope, and living bread for those who hunger for hope. The origin for this hope is in simple, human touch, not superheroes. Touch is experiential. We can feel touch. We feel the touch that is tactile when we are hugged, and we feel the touch that is non-tactile when a passage of music touches our hearts. Touch is cognitive when an idea touches our imagination, and thrills and excites us with novelty and creativity. A kind and supportive word from our spouse or partner when we are going through a trying situation at work, touches our soul with gentle fingers, prompting us to tear up, sigh, or whisper, "I love you." Countless are the ways in which touch mends, and uplifts.

We live in an age that wants to be in touch. We desire to be in touch with our deepest dimensions. Some call that depth the heart, while others may name it our soul. Our innermost regions, or our deepest self, are the dwelling place of meaning, purpose, identity, and communion with others and the Greatest Mystery. For the moment, it appears that we have misplaced the map to our deeper self, and are ransacking our desk, and house to locate it.

We desire to be in touch with those who matter the most to us. Our intimate others—parents, spouses, partners, children, relatives, and dear friends—lack the warmth of our loving and caring touch. We live in the same house, sit at the same table, and yet are out of touch with the very ones to whom we are the closest. We want to be attached to our intimate others, and want them to be attached to us—a relationship where we mutually matter to one another.

It takes time to build relationships. Ordinary moments are the building blocks of empathy and rapport. Routine interactions at the end of the school day, or workday, open doors where feelings of sorrow, joy, apprehension, and pride are greeted with a hug. Working together around the house plants seeds that give rise to the trust required for another to express their hurts and hopes.

We are out of touch with nature. The sense that we are part of creation, itself a dynamic biosphere in which we were birthed, is an endangered concept and perspective. We are detached, far more than attached, to Mother Earth. We act like we are the owners of this planet, rather than the stewards with a significant responsibility for its well-being. The appreciation that earth nourishes and sustains us by its gifts of gravity, water, oxygen, sunlight, and nutrients is evaporating in the heat of our ill-advised insensitivity and self-absorption.

Our utter disregard for the planet and its delicate, and dynamic web of interconnections is irrational, and threatens our species and other life-forms, animate and inanimate. Bodies of water are evaporating. Oceans are warming. Ice packs are melting. The planet's surface is heating up. The fossil remains of life-forms that failed to adapt to their climate are now fueling the very toxic gases and by-products that are asphyxiating and poisoning us, and the planet. Earth has been around a long time, and will persist. We are welcome to travel along as it orbits around the sun, as long as we behave as appreciative passengers. Earth's patience is wearing thin.

Friends are irreplaceable, knowing us better than anyone else, and whom we completely trust. Our closest friends know our quirks and shortcomings, and still love us. Friends are the ones who hold us accountable, and confront us when our words, thoughts, or actions are not in our best interest, nor of benefit to others. These confrontations from our friends are rooted in love, sparked by a commitment to our well-being, and to the friendship.

Friends seek to cultivate those traits that help us be our best, and to hold in check the undesirable aspects of our personality. This give-and-take among and between friends requires effort. Such honest dialogue is a feature of an ongoing friendship, one traveling over time, being forged by disagreements and disappointments, forgiveness, shared joys, and celebrations, thereby hammering and fashioning strong bonds on friendship's anvil.

Neighbors are important to our lives, touching us with their concern, and interest in us. To be in touch with our neighbor is to extend respect, courtesy, and consideration. Being in touch with our neighbors means that there is some attachment, some compassion and empathy.

Compassion and empathy for the life circumstances of other fellow human beings in our neighborhood, city, nation, or foreign country, require that we are in touch with their humanity. Being in touch contributes to the establishment of an attachment to another person or people. This attachment makes it possible to care about them. Given a diminished, or a lack of, attachment among and between neighbors, the neighbor-to-neighbor relationship is compromised. As communities across our land, and as a nation, we have lost touch with the humanity of those who are our neighborhood—national and international neighbors.

Tribes signal a loss of touch with the colorful variety of people on our streets, in our nation, and around the globe. Tribes by their nature are exclusive, and highly protective of what they consider "theirs." Tribes replace neighbors with people who are "just like us, the same as us!" People collect in tribes, cohering with those who are like them, most particularly in terms of politics, culture, race, and worldviews. Tribes generate this type of language: "People outside our tribe are 'them,' those who are different, not like us. Since they are not like us, we do not like them, and we have little empathy or compassion for them."

This contemporary division of people into "us" and "them" puts us out of touch with our common humanity with all people. For example, all people have hopes and dreams. They know success and failure. They love, and are loved. They are buffeted by powers not of their own making, and are subject to their gene pool. Prejudice and bias may open or shut doors for them, depending on culture, sexual orientation, gender, nationality, religion, or position. Our sense of the wonderful variety, and the amazing commonality of people, are what allow us to be in touch with our neighbors—whoever and wherever they are.

We also yearn to be in touch with the Sacred. The number of books and magazines on spirituality, and the interest in mindfulness, yoga, meditation, and reflection point to this interest. While more attention appears to be given to the traditions of the East particularly, there are rich resources as well in Christianity, Judaism, and Islam that speak to the quest to be in touch with the Sacred. These pursuits of the Sacred, and these involvements in spirituality, engage seekers in healthy and beneficial activities.

On the other hand, another segment of our culture senses an intense inner emptiness, which alerts them to the reality that there is more to life than they are currently experiencing. Wincing with the unbearable pain of an agonizing emptiness, people turn to screens, sex, substances, and possessions ("stuff") to forget, or at least numb, their pain. They develop addictions to these activities. Sadly, the addictions are unsuccessful in abating the pain of emptiness and fail to grant access to the "more" in life, of which people are confident exists, yet is painfully absent.

SIGNIFICANCE OF TOUCH

The human experience of touch begins when the female egg and the male sperm embrace. It is the egg that opens its outer layer, allowing entrance to one sperm. The egg opens its door to this sperm, and then closes that door to all other sperm. Once that sperm is welcomed, the egg becomes impenetrable. That embrace begins a journey, where the now fertilized egg, the zygote, takes up residence in the womb, where human life continues its blossoming. The fertilized egg attaches itself to the wall of the uterus. Attachment is the essence of human life, for in short order, the fetus and the uterus will be attached via the umbilical cord. Our navel ("belly button") is a lifelong reminder of this life-giving attachment.

As the fetus evolves, and organs begin to form, the largest human organ envelopes the fetus in a protective shield: the skin. Senses begin to appear—sight, sound, taste, and touch. Of all the human senses, touch is identified as the first to be present. Touch and attachment are companions. Touch is a key component of how we establish attachments. Attachments frequently require touch, and touching. Attachment and touch are far warmer concepts and realities than "connections," an overused, and misused term in today's discourse.

Touch and attachment are how we are created. Humans are a phenomenon of relationships. The primal relationship is that of the Greatest Mystery of Life uniting itself with matter. Matter and Spirit touch, and begin that joyful dance we term "Life." Life itself is a manifestation of relating, from the embrace of the egg and sperm, to fetus in utero, floating in an embryonic body of fluid, to the relationship of the fetus to the mother for life-giving O2 and nutrients. This relationship is the union of Spirit and matter.

Touch gives us life. Touch is life, being as essential as oxygen, water, and nourishment. Touch joins us to others. It helps commune, be one. It is communication itself. It speaks its own language.[1] Touch can express thoughts and feelings, at times speaking what words are unable to say. Touch affects our thinking, as well as our moods. An empathetic touch can help us find a solution to a baffling problem, and a caring touch can soothe our troubled hearts, while buoying our sinking spirits.[2]

A poignant example of a profoundly stirring touch occurred in a court room in 2019. In that courtroom, the jury had returned a guilty verdict of manslaughter for the female police officer, Amber Guyger, who shot to death a man, Botham Jean, in his own apartment. She mistook the man's apartment as her own, and thinking him an intruder, killed him with gunfire. The nation was shocked and outraged.

The man's family, of course, was present for the trial. One of the family members present on the final day was the deceased's younger brother. When he completed his testimony about his brother, he turned in the witness stand to face the judge, and asked, "May I give the defendant a hug?" The judge was silent. A second time the question was posed, "May I give the defendant a hug?" The judge said, "Yes."

The brother rose from his chair in the witness stand, and descended to the courtroom floor. He then strode to the defendant, who had stepped away from the defendant's table. They met in front of the judge, and the brother gave her a warm embrace. Both were crying. The flow of reconciling, forgiving, caring power from the brother to the police officer was tangible, visible in the shaking of her shoulders as she was held. Pictures of the hug were carried by the major news networks.

1. Keltner, "Hands On Research."
2. Keltner, "Hands On Research."

Incredibly, the judge left the bench, and likewise gave the defendant a hug. She also gave the police officer a Bible. This hug was also broadcast broadly throughout the nation.

Touch is the essence of life. Touch is essential for life: that is its significance. Nothing lives in a vacuum. Living is a relational phenomenon. We are creatures of relationships, that is, attachments.

While "relationship," and "attachment" are all but synonymous, there is a distinction to be made. Relationships are given, and are more of a factuality than a quality. A relationship is a fact, as in a father and his son. The quality of that relationship is a question of the dimension of attachment. Attachments require relationships, yet are more about the quality of that relationship. That is, is the attachment nourishing? Two students may be related as classmates, yet inquiry is required to determine how important they are to one another.

We are wired to relate. Humans, like other organic life forms, are a constellation of relationships. In physiological terms, humans are relationships of cells, tissue, nerve pathways and synapses, muscles, systems of circulation, digestion, elimination, respiration. These relationships are in symphony with one another, each depending on the other in the intricate dance that constitutes life.

Touch consists of both being a part of and being apart from. Restated, touch is a continuum where we are attached (a part of), and simultaneously differentiated (apart from). As the egg and sperm are apart from one another, they attach to begin a complex, intricate, and delicate process of differentiation. The end result of the in utero process is a being that consists of distinct cells, organs, and systems, which all are in concert with one another to form a whole that is greater than the sum of its parts: a human. Once outside the womb, the fetus, now a baby, earlier a part of its mother via the umbilical cord, has that cord severed, thereby becoming apart from the mother.

This process of being a part of and apart from is basic to touch. We strive to be a part of without being swallowed up, and to be apart from in a manner that does not isolate or detach us from others. For us to be attached to others involves a balance of a part of and apart from. Our attachments are the way we are in touch with others, and how they are in touch with us.

Touch is reciprocal: what we touch touches us. Touch is always mutual: the toucher and the touched become one. We seek to achieve individuation, and avoid alienation.

Attachments speak to the element of affection and value we have for others. Attachment has to do with the bonds that are in place between people. Our attachments are what steady and ground us. For persons who have tenuous attachments, there is a sense of being adrift, and a lack of security. Psychology realizes the significance of attachments in its theories and concepts of human well-being, particularly the Bowlby attachment theory.[3]

Family therapy, as seen in the work of Salvador Minuchin, MD, discusses and demonstrates the importance of members of the family system being a part of, while also being apart from, the family. A family member is to avoid being too close or too removed from the family system.[4]

Another family therapist, theorist, and clinician, Murray Bowen, MD, talks about a healthy family system, and accordingly, healthy individuals, in terms of "individuated" and "enmeshed." The individuated person is a distinct and differentiated individual, with clear boundaries between the person and the family. The "enmeshed" person has a greatly diminished sense of self, and such diffuse boundaries that the person's thoughts and feelings are generated more by the family than by the individual.[5]

The mental health diagnostic guide the *Diagnostic and Statistical Manual 5* (*DSM-5*), describes the problems that are attributable to the lack, or disruption, of healthy attachments. Some of these problems are "excessive fear and anxiety."[6] Other behaviors may appear, such as "social withdrawal, apathy, sadness, or difficulty concentrating."[7]

---

3. Bowlby, *Attachment and Loss*.

4. Minuchin, *Families and Family Therapy*; Bowen, *Family Therapy*.

5 Bowen, *Family Therapy*.

6. *DSM-5*, 191.

7. *DSM-5*, 192.

The centrality of relating extends beyond humans to the world of nature. Nature is the biosphere in which humans, along with other life forms, are birthed. The interior world of human life is dependent on the world outside our skin, a world we name Nature. Human life requires being in touch with earth's oxygen, gravity, sunlight, foods. Our nostrils, eyes, mouths, ears are gateways through which oxygen, nourishment, and sights and sounds are welcomed.

Touch likewise allows the world to imprint its beauty and grandeur on us. Beyond the basic requirement we have for oxygen, water, sunlight, and food, we also require from nature those phenomena that inspire, soothe, bewilder, delight, and amaze us.

Touch is a social reality. Humans are created to live in a context, familial, social, and cultural. Our environment of others is essential to the emergence, development, and nurturing of what we call the Self. There is no "I" without a "We." In the womb, the fetus begins a journey of individuation while related.

During its unfolding, the fetus takes on its individuality, doing so while intimately related to its mother. When the infant sucks in the first breath of oxygen on its own, it extends its relationship beyond its mother, and to the larger world beyond it.

At birth, the infant enters another galaxy of relationships, where its journey of individuation continues in its myriad interactions with others and the world. The process of individuation leads to the development of an independent human, an "I." This "I" encounters other differentiated individuals, and begins to learn how to create basic relationships of "you and me," which now forms a third constellation, that of the "We," or the "Us." So, it is that individuals coevolve as both an "I," and a "We."

The emergence of the self-in-relationship includes the world of emotions. We touch the hearts, minds, and spirits of those around us. Our words touch another person with affection. The caring expression on our face offers a touch of support to our friend's heart. Our hand on the shoulder of a work colleague is a touch of admiration for her or his contributions to the work team. A card on our loved one's birthday, inscribed with a brief note, is a warm and caring touch. Slowing down to allow a vehicle to merge into our lane is a courteous touch to the other driver.

The extent to which we touch the hearts and minds of others is frequently unknown to us. On those occasions when someone tells us what a difference we made in their lives; we are surprised. To us, we were simply doing our daily, ordinary things: going to work, saying "hello," listening when someone wants to talk, taking the kids to music lessons, having dinner with the family, texting a friend, spending time with our beloved—nothing special; merely every-day routines. Then, unexpectedly, we are amazed when someone tells us how we touched their lives. A student we had in our class tells us at a class reunion what an imprint we made on their lives. A neighbor tells us how much it meant that we came over when the ambulance arrived to rush a family member to the hospital. A person at work we know in passing, tells us how months ago, our simple smile and good morning greeting lifted them from a dark hole. One of our longtime bank customers tells us how steadying and comforting we were as we helped him sort through bank records and accounts following the death of his spouse.

A member of the congregation tells me years later how one of my sermons set him to thinking about a career change that took him down a path of fulfillment. His name was Clay, and he had recently retired. Now, he was wondering what to do in his retirement. One Sunday, I preached a sermon on the future, and how God places before us new paths to heretofore unseen promised lands. Clay told me that at that point, his mind began to wonder about fresh possibilities for his life. He concluded that real estate was his new career, and he became quite successful in it. Until he told me this story, I had no idea how I touched him.

In our world of relationships, our physical presence, our words, moods, behaviors, body posture, facial expression, and more are all imprinting the lives of myriad others. We cannot not touch other people, nor are we able to avoid being touched by others. Touch is the world we inhabit.

While I was the director of chaplaincy services at Presbyterian Hospital in Albuquerque, I was the only ancillary, and nonclinical, member on a committee charged with the oversight of clinicians' performance and conduct, the Professional Standards Overview Committee. One of the cases that came to this committee for consideration concerned an emergency department patient. The patient, a teenage male, was seen by a clinician. He was brought in by his mother, complaining of stomach pain and nausea. After examining the boy, the clinician sent the boy home in the care of his mother, along with some antacids. They were instructed to call the ED or return if the symptoms worsened.

The next day, the boy showed back up in the emergency department running a fever and in great discomfort. Another diagnosis was performed, and this time a ruptured appendix was discovered, along with sepsis throughout his body. He was hospitalized, but it was too late. He died soon after.

The original clinician was found to have performed a proper diagnosis—"by the book." Teenage boys with an inflamed appendix are difficult to diagnosis. It is not unusual, I learned, for a teenage male with abdominal pain to be sent home with antacids, with instructions to phone or return if the symptoms worsen. The clinician was assured that her professional performance was not being questioned.

Her emergency department colleagues and friends did their best to comfort her. Nonetheless, she was in agony, filled with self-doubt and self-blame. After the committee's meeting, she and I had some conversations during which I listened, comforted, and supported her in my role as a chaplain. After those conversations, I had no further contact with her.

Some years later, I got a phone call while I was at my desk in the hospital. The caller gave me her name, but I did not recognize her. Then she said, "I am the clinician that you talked to following the death of the teenage boy with appendicitis." "Oh," I said, a bit embarrassed that I did not recognize her name. "How are things with you?" "Well," she replied, "that is why I called." "After you and I had our talks, I read every journal article on teenage boy appendicitis that I could find. I talked to physicians, and to other nurse practitioners. I left no stone unturned in my efforts to see if I should have done something different. What I learned from my research was that I observed the standards of care." "That is an amazing effort on your part," I said. "I hope that your discovery offers you some relief." She commented, "Yes, it does. You can see that it was a journey of years for me to arrive at this place. I want you to know how important our talks were. I was so down and was being so hard on myself that I was ready to quit medicine. You helped me remain in medicine, which is what I genuinely love." You could have knocked me over with a feather.

In like manner, we are surprised, and often shocked, when others tell us of the pain we caused them. Our coworker tells us how what we said hurt them. Our beloved tells us the look on our face over dinner made them feel like they had done something wrong. The clerk at the checkout stand tells us we are being rude when we question an item on the receipt. Our child begins to cry when we ask how things went at school.

Unknown to us, we touch others in ways that bring pain. We had no intent to be rude or appear harsh. What we said or did was nothing unusual in our mind. Our wish was to be curious, or supportive, and learn to the contrary, that we were experienced as being critical or controlling. We may have been preoccupied about work while having dinner, somewhat withdrawn, and learn we were perceived as being angry or bored. These moments remind us that the touch others experience is frequently not the touch we intend to impart.

On occasion, we are so caught up in ourselves that we purposely withhold touch from others. We may sense that a touch (word, expression, hug) would help another, and we determine that we will not offer that kindness. We may be so self-absorbed that we are deaf and blind to those around us, concerned more with ourselves than others who would welcome, or even need, acknowledgment. Looking in a mirror complicates seeing anyone other than ourselves.

Touch is life-nourishing, or life-shrinking. A life-nourishing touch is a kind, supportive, or encouraging word. It may be a facial expression, or it may be a hug or pat on the shoulder that says, "I care."

Life-shrinking touch ranges from one that takes another's physical life, to a touch that is effacing, hobbling, and diminishes someone's emotional, mental, and spiritual life. Many a person knows the pain of life-shrinking touch. This harmful touch certainly is physical or verbal, or may be one inflicted by social media. Some people are highly guarded about touching others, and certainly about being touched. Keeping up their guard, a sizable number of people minimize touching, or avoid it all together.

Destructive touch has many forms that channel overpowering violence and disregard. People are raped. Some are beaten. Adults and children are bullied at work or school, and over the internet. Sexual and physical assaults batter people's body, mind, and spirit. Psychological assault whittles away at a person's sense of worth.

In relationships where there is a power differential, people are subjected to exploitative and tumultuous touch by the very person whom they trusted to be a caring and helpful resource. We find ourselves betrayed by the one we trusted with our bodies, minds, or spirits to help us. It may be a member of the clergy, a physician, a professor, a therapist, or a schoolteacher, who in truth is a predator, not a professional. It is common for us to experience similar violations from relatives, friends, or neighbors. Such ruinous touches leave wounds that persist over a lifetime.

While attending Vanderbilt's School of Divinity in Nashville, I was the chaplain at the Junior League Crippled Children's Home. Every Sunday a member of a local Protestant church came by to visit the children, followed by my leading the children in some age- and developmentally-appropriate activities.

One Sunday, when my wife and I arrived at the home, I found the nursing staff distraught, highly agitated, angry, and sad. I was informed that one of the teenage boys who had profound cerebral palsy had been molested by the Protestant visitor. The boy used an alphabet board to communicate. While the cerebral palsy robbed him of the ability to walk and talk, it left his fine mind intact. The nursing staff was incredulous as he used his alphabet board to recount what happened to him.

When a physical exam of the boy was conducted by the nurses, all doubt was removed. Now their incredulity became anger: "What kind of man does that to a defenseless boy?" Sorrow also appeared: "I am heartbroken for this boy, our patient."

We know the distinction between a light touch and a heavy-handed touch. We compliment those musicians whose fingers seem to float over piano keys or cello strings, saying that these artists have such a light touch. On occasion when we require medical or nursing care, we know health care professionals who exhibit a light touch when drawing blood or helping us adjust our position in bed. There are those administrators in our work and professional lives who use a light touch when necessary as they coach us on how to improve our performance. During our childhood, we experienced the light touch of our parents as they talked with us about how our current behavior could lead to disadvantageous consequences.

We can recount moments when a heavy hand touched our lives. Some supervisors and administrators treated us with a steel hand in a velvet glove, bluntly telling us how inadequate and incapable we were. Health care professionals delivered diagnostic results in an insensitive manner, while others were rough and clumsy with procedures.

Some years ago, I was involved in a propane fire, which burned over 23 percent of my body with second- and third-degree burns. I was hospitalized for a month, underwent twice a day debridings in a tub, and had surgery to place skin grafts on my burns.

I learned a lot about touch. For instance, I could feel the individual fibers of the towel used to dry me. I asked if the towels were starched, or were of a stiffer composition for use on the burn unit. "No," was the reply. "They are simple, everyday, run-of-the-mill towels." I was miserable.

Since my hands and arms were burned, I required a bit more nursing care. I did feed myself, as part of my physical therapy, and to keep my fingers flexible. For almost everything else, I required a nurse.

I and the nurses got well acquainted. It did not take me long to learn who had a soft touch, and who had a hard touch. I learned the nurse's work schedules, and knew who would be on duty on what day. One nurse, who generally worked the night shift, was heavy handed. She was not mean. Her touch was rough, her grip like a vise, her positioning of me clumsy. I prayed for her to be gentle with me.

Some of us had a parent who behaved more like the proverbial drill sergeant in telling us in a no-holds-barred manner to clean up our act—or else. Not only have we been the recipient of a heavy-handed touch, but we also know that we have used a heavy-handed touch in relating to others. These memories may be a source of regret or embarrassment, generating thoughts of "I wish I had handled that better."

When touch is respectful and caring, it amazes us with its power to weave our lives together with others. Life knits us together through touch, and through touch we weave ourselves into relationships with others. Weaving intertwines us to our beloved, giving us the sense of being one with our beloved. As we mutually weave this relationship, the distinct threads of our two lives maintain their uniqueness while simultaneously fashioning a basket, capable of containing the relationship. This basket is greater than the sum of its parts.

This level of interwoven touch lets us know that we matter. A significant component of human well-being is the awareness that we make a difference to others. This awareness is reciprocal. The mutuality of being cherished is the experience that while other people matter to us, they in turn cherish us. This relationship of cherishing and being cherished fills us with the profound sense of how much life matters to us. We discover that we matter to life, for in the world of our cherished other, we contribute significantly to that person's sense that she or he matters. We are both recipient and granter of the essential experience of being esteemed. There is no more mournful and dark despair than concluding that we are of no consequence. This plaintive and painful despair is joined by the conclusion that Life itself has no attraction or meaning. The lost sense that we are esteemed, and that Life itself is unimportant are the origins of apathy, seclusion, loneliness, depression, and suicide. It matters that we matter.

THE SPIRITUAL SELF AND TOUCH

AWE, WONDER, AND TOUCH

I invite you to join me in a conversation about God, or as I shall reference the Divine, the "Greatest Mystery." The term "Greatest Mystery" is as an acknowledgment that God has no name. To name God is a presumption to have the power to define and describe, even understand that which is ineffable and impenetrable. The closest to a name for the Greatest Mystery is the phrase "I am," a term employed by the Deity in Jewish and Christian scriptures.

The following prayer eloquently states how incomprehensible, transcendent, and yet accessible is the Eternal. It depicts the Greatest Mystery as near and far, as transcendent, and immanent, unknowable, and personal, and as origin and destiny.

> *O God who transcends all.*
> *How can we call you by any name?*
> *What hymn of praise can we sing of you?*
> *No name can describe you.*
> *What mind can grasp you?*
> *No intellect can conceive you.*
> *You are beyond words;*
> *Yet all that is spoken comes from you.*
> *You are unknowable;*
> *And yet all thought comes from you.*
> *All creatures praise you,*
> *Both those who speak and those that are dumb.*

All creatures bow down before you,
Both those who can think and those that cannot.
The longing of the universe,
The groaning of creation reaches out to you.
Everything that exists prays to you,
And every creature that can read your universe
Directs to you a hymn of silence.
In you alone do all things exist.
All things find their goal in you;
You are the destiny of every creature.
You are unique.
You dwell in all but are not any.
You are not an individual creature,
Nor are you the sum of your creatures;
All names are yours; so how shall I address you,
You alone who cannot be named?
O God who transcends all, have mercy;
How can we call you by any name?[1]

The most profound human experience of touch is the ex-perience of being touched by the Greatest Mystery. The Greatest Mystery is that which transcends us, is greater than we, is the Alpha and Omega, beginning and completion, of all the cosmos. This Greatest Mystery, the Summa Mystery, is the sense that there is "More" in and to life. It is our spiritual self's awareness of the Holy Other, one in which we experience a depthless presence. This experience is the sense of union, or comm-union, meaning "union with," or, a being one with the Greatest Mystery.

We have, in varying degrees, sadly lost touch with our spiri-tual self. How do we lose touch with our spiritual self? How do we lose touch with the indwelling of the Spirit in us? How do we lose touch with the union of Spirit and matter? After all, the Greatest Mystery inhabits all creation, and that includes us. The Greatest Mystery's presence is a given, not something we have to seek.

There is a beauty in the Greatest Mystery's finding us, and in our seeking the Greatest Mystery. This seeking is mutually

---

1. A reading from the *Dogmatic Poems* of Gregory of Nazianzus, quoted in Atwell, *Celebrating the Seasons*, 342.

reciprocal. Restated, the Greatest Mystery seeks us, while we find the Greatest Mystery. This dynamic, even paradox, of being sought by the Greatest Mystery, and our seeking the Greatest Mystery, is a both/and. There is no contradiction.

In Psalms 145 we are taught to seek God with sincerity. In Psalm 139, we learn that God's hand leads and holds the worshipper regardless of the worshipper's location or situation. We seek the Greatest Mystery. The Greatest Mystery seeks us. It is as though we are dancers, each reaching for the hand of the other, of the partner.

In the womb, the Greatest Mystery is the animating power of life, making life the result of a union of Spirit and matter. Spirit, as the creative power, infuses all creation. We find it in our inner world, and in our outer world, in our interior, and in nature.

We lose touch with our spiritual self, and lose touch with the sense of the indwelling of the Spirit by submitting to the world's insistence that only the concrete, measurable world is real. We buy into the view that objects, numbers, and things are the only reality. All else is an illusion.

This world of objects and things has no room for the Transcendent, for that which is real, yet is not measurable. That which is not measurable is real. For instance, how do you measure your love for music or your desire to write poetry? How do you measure your love for your spouse, a love that is real and takes form in words and deeds, behaviors, and conversations? How about patriotism, known as "love of country": is that measurable? A sizable segment of the population would offer military service as a reliable measure of patriotism. Is patriotism likewise measured by the devotion of a school teacher to her or his students, by the dedication and courage of first responders, of the commitment of those serving in the many branches and levels of our judiciary, or by protesters seeking a more just society and world?

Losing touch with that which transcends us, and which cannot be quantified, comes with a heavy price. That price is our willingness to strip bare the verdant meadow of human experience, with its beauty, flowers, scents, insects, streams, birds, animals, colors, and make it a barren and stark desert. We voluntarily, and unwisely, lose touch with our spiritual self, thereby lessening, if not excluding, our experiences of wonder and awe. The wonder and awe remain, and abound. However, we have eyes that do not see, and ears that do not hear all the marvel surrounding us.

This manufactured picture that only what is measurable is real is a house of sticks. As such, it is unable to withstand the torrents and currents of life which have more than enough power to sweep aside what is a flimsy structure. In like manner, as a house of sticks, we are able through our own efforts of thought and deed to cause the house of sticks to wobble and tumble. Whether this manufactured and false construct of reality is dismantled by the winds or tides of life, or by an individual's deliberate initiative, it is possible to see the light of the Transcendent shining through the cracks.

That crack in the façade of the house of sticks may appear in a moment of beauty, or tragedy. The crack may begin and spread its thin lines in a moment of keen sorrow, or one of exuberant joy. A small sliver of light may find a pinhole opening in a moment of exhaustion, or a time of exhilaration. Perhaps illness or a loss will cause us to squint our eyes as a novel shaft of light pierces the darkness of our situation. Another reality may be glimpsed in a moment of awe, or a time of "sheer silence."

It is these moments at the peaks and valleys of experience, when the Greatest Mystery is beheld through the thin veil, that the world of the Greatest Mystery and the spiritual self are known to be real. The walls of materialism's citadel crumble and fall, revealing it for the human construct that it is. In its place stands the equally real power and presence of the Greatest Mystery, that which is greater than we, and sets limits and opens portals of possibility. What is this "greater" reality?

To answer this question requires an in-depth exploration of the metaphorical nature of touch. By and large, this book attends to the importance of metaphorical touch. I talk about what touches the heart, or what touches the soul. Chapter 7, "Relationships and Touch," will talk about healing touch, and harmful touch, weaving together physical touch and metaphorical touch, in a manner that demonstrates the extraordinary power of physical touch to have an impact on the heart, soul, and mind.

The "greater" of which I speak is the experience of being touched by the Greatest Mystery. The Greatest Mystery is

> that which envelopes and permeates the cosmos, of-
> fering new possibilities, setting limits, instigating new
> beginnings, establishing endings, and creating in us
> dispositions of wonder and awe, humility, gratitude, re-
> sponsibility, courage, and fulfillment.

What we require as individuals and as communities is a spiritual awakening, one in which we accept the gift of being touched by the Greatest Mystery. This awakening is foundational to our restoring touch in our lives, touch with the Greatest Mystery, self, others, Mother Earth. It is my hope that this book may play some role in that awakening.

When we experience the touch of the Greatest Mystery, we are embraced by wonder and awe, realizing there is that which is greater than we. We are not the author of our own being. All of life, including us, is a gift. Acknowledging this gift fills us with amazement, humility, and gratitude. These gifts come unmerited, and place upon us a responsibility. We are stewards, not owners. We are caretakers, not stockholders.

The basis of our ability to touch and be in touch is attributable to the reality-altering experience of the Greatest Mystery first touching us. We can touch because we have been touched. How do we respond to the sacred touch? Do we flinch, draw back, run? Do we return the touch, first taking a hand, then hugging, followed by embracing? This embrace, this hug, this hand-holding is lifelong, far from a polite "How do you do?" and then stepping back, ending the touch. No, when we respond to the touch of the Greatest Mystery with an embrace, then we can embrace ourselves, others, and the planet. We become attached to our inner world of self and to the world beyond us. This capacity to touch and create attachments is a gift granted us.

There is a root anxiety in humans which leads to a rejection of the touch of the Greatest Mystery. This basic anxiety strives to protect and advance the self-interest of the individual, a people, or a nation. Some expressions of this root anxiety are selfishness, bigotry, or nationalism. Unless a person can find in the Greatest Mystery certainty and stability, that person will resort to their own devices, and generally destructive devices, to advance their cause.

We are a spiritual being, with a spiritual self and center. Our spiritual self, and our spirituality are part of our DNA. The Greatest Mystery breathes Spirit into us at creation. Spirit is present in the womb, as Spirit and matter are coalesced in our shaping and forming. Spirit then is the essential life force. The life-giving Spirit of the Greatest Mystery is not a foreign entity, but a welcome and vital component of human life.

All living things are energized by the breath, or Spirit of God. Spirit and breath are the same term, translated differently. The interior of animals and humans becomes a dwelling place for God's breath, Spirit, or life-power. Indeed, the Greatest Mystery shares a common concern and valuation for these two Spirit-bearing creations: "Your righteousness is like the mighty mountains, your judgments are like the great deep; you save humans and animals alike, O Lord" (Ps 36:6 NRSV).

The Spirit of the Greatest Mystery is the source of all creation. In the book of Genesis, the creating power of the Greatest Mystery's Spirit (breath) moves over the formless deep, calling forth order to replace the chaos. The Greatest Mystery's breath then is the creating, ordering, sustaining, renewing, and novelty-establishing power of all reality. This cosmos-creating power is breathed into humans and animals. The Greatest Mystery's Spirit is an indwelling presence.

The Greatest Mystery's interior presence in humans is a given. The Greatest Mystery is not so much found, as acknowledged. It is already present and available. There is no need to hunt for what is at hand.

Listening, not hunting, is the approach to take when seeking the presence of the Greatest Mystery. The great prophet Elijah fled for his life to a cave on Mount Horeb (1 Kgs 19:8ff.). Queen Jezebel intended to kill him for slaying all the royal prophets with a sword.

Elijah spoke and acted on behalf of the Greatest Mystery, and now felt quite alone facing Jezebel's threat.

The Eternal One inquires of Elijah, "What are you doing here . . . ?" Basically, Elijah says that he is all alone, and that he fears for his life. From this dialogue, it is clear that Elijah and the Greatest Mystery are in conversation, but Elijah does not feel connected, or in touch, with the Greatest Mystery.

Elijah is instructed to go stand on the mountain, as the Greatest Mystery is about to pass by. A great wind arose, one so strong that it split rocks. The Greatest Mystery was not in that wind. An earthquake came next, and the Greatest Mystery was not in the earthquake. Next came a mighty fire, and the Greatest Mystery was not in the fire. After the fire was the "sound of sheer silence," and Elijah heard it. Imagine listening with such intensity and clarity that you can hear the "sound of sheer silence"!

In this drama of the Greatest Mystery seeking to connect with Elijah, and Elijah making a personal effort to hear again the voice of the Greatest Mystery, we see simultaneously the extension of two hands, each reaching for the other. With Elijah standing on the mountain as commanded to listen and discern, and with the Greatest Mystery providing "sheer silence," their communication was reestablished.

Likewise, the Greatest Mystery's Spirit, as the creative power, is in all creation, animate and inanimate. Animals and humans have the same Spirit, and all that flies, walks, swims, creeps, crawls, climbs, or slithers is called into life by the Spirit. Rivers, planets, stars, mountains, oceans, and deserts are also shaped and formed by the creating Spirit. Thus, we may find God in our interior world, and in our outer world; in our inner, subjective self, and in the objective, external world of nature.

This relationship of Spirit and matter is one of harmony and mutuality, not one of oil and water. Flesh, human and animal, is inseparably interwoven with the breath of the Greatest Mystery. When the Greatest Mystery's breath departs from humans or animals, they die. Death is the departure of the Greatest Mystery's indwelling animating Breath-presence.

We do nothing to gain or attain the experience of encountering the Greatest Mystery: it is given to us. We receive this experience, and are benefactors in the interaction. Like Elijah, we need to be in the right "place" in our lives and listen carefully to discern the "sheer silence" the Greatest Mystery offers, what we call an "ah-ha" moment. The more technical term is a *theophany*, or the appearance and awareness of the Greatest Mystery.

This experience is a coming to consciousness of what has been true of us since our conception, i.e., the Eternal resides in us. From conception, you are one with the Greatest Mystery. The Greatest Mystery is in all, and through all. In the Greatest Mystery, you live, move, and have your being.

The question is not the absence or presence of the Greatest Mystery. The question is more how perceptive and aware are we of that presence? Human perception is not the best on the planet. Other animals hear more and better, see more and better, and sense more and better than we. Nevertheless, our senses of awareness and perception are suited to our needs as humans. We possess all the intellectual power, intuitive power, and the power of perception in the broadest sense to be aware of the Greatest Mystery. Our task is to have a clear mind, a discerning Spirit, and an open heart so that we might be cognizant of the Greatest Mystery.

MARVEL AND TOUCH

In our experience of the Greatest Mystery, awe and wonder are foremost. It is the nature of the Greatest Mystery to reach out and touch us. When we are touched by the Greatest Mystery, our immediate response is that of awe. The awe is generated by our awareness that there is that which is greater than we. There are powers, limits, possibilities, wonders, conditions, circumstances, forces, givens, and mysteries, all which vastly exceed and dwarf human capabilities and conceptions.

Such an awareness of that which is greater than we may occur while standing on a beach, staring out across an endless stretch of an ocean. The Greatest Mystery may touch us as we gaze upon the

Grand Canyon, amazed by the geological wonders fashioned over eons by a flowing river. We may be mesmerized as we gaze into the face of our newborn infant, smiling and cooing, fresh from its mother's womb, full of life, and an amazing marvel to behold. Spellbound, the Greatest Mystery may reveal itself to us with blazing colors of autumn—yellow, orange, and red flames. We stare in amazement at a spider's web holding captive the sun's rays in its intricate and delicate web. A blossom of spring entrances us, for this beacon of color and warmth follows the colorless and cold autumn—amazing!

These fresh experiences of the Greatest Mystery are often routine, simple, everyday events and moments. However, the thin veil is pulled back, and these common moments shed their everyday garb and become more than ordinary. They become picture windows allowing us to see what is always present: that there is a transcendent power about us, a power that towers above our limited human capacities of mind, muscle, and will. This power offers us possibilities, and intends for us to live life well, full, and abundantly. This power and energy reside in us, awaiting our discovery.

Take a rainbow, for instance. Rainbows are a natural phenomenon for which we have a scientific explanation. It is not supernatural by any means, with the same being true for total eclipses of the sun and moon. Here in New Mexico, we often are treated to double rainbows. When is a rainbow not a common rainbow? A rainbow is not "just another rainbow" when it fills you with awe. The awe is not based on a lack of understanding of the rainbow's appearance. To the contrary, the awe moves from the presence or absence of understanding, to the dimension of amazement. The rainbow gives us pause. We stop our car, and take a picture. We are hypnotized. We are entranced. The rainbow is no longer a phenomenon of optics, color spectrum, light, water, prisms, physics. It now is a marvel. It is transformed. We are transformed. Our wonder finds its voice in exclamations: "Isn't that beautiful?—wow!"

In such moments of wonder and awe, as we experience the Greatest Mystery, we sense a oneness with all creation. The Greatest Mystery envelopes us, always present, occasionally glimpsed.

Some say that a thin veil separates our routine world, and the world of something more. These thin places may be designated as fixed sites of the sacred: temples, shrines, sanctuaries, or holy ground. Thin places may be happenstance: an airport, beach, city park, a kitchen table. Or they may be a rare natural phenomenon, such as a total eclipse of the sun or moon. Those who participate in these events find them deeply moving, with some describing it as movingly spiritual.

The experience of the Greatest Mystery can occur in routine conversation and interaction. This kaleidoscopic-like event occurs when common interactions with another person are metamorphized, transformed. How this transformation happens is elusive, and fills us with awe. What we do know is that suddenly, in our interaction with another person, something bigger than both of us is present.

Recently I attended a retreat on joy. The leader of the retreat used the book *The Book of Joy: Lasting Happiness in a Changing World*, by His Holiness the Dalai Lama and Archbishop Desmond Tutu, with Douglas Abrams (Avery Press, 2016). We had been instructed to bring journals or notebooks to do some reflection and writing throughout the day.

The workshop was stimulating. We explored the nature of joy, the obstacles to joy, and the pillars of joy. I used my notebook to reflect and write as the leader directed us, and occasionally took a note on something she was highlighting. It was a good day.

At some point in discussing the obstacles to joy, I raised the question of purpose, my purpose specifically. Since retirement, I saw myself as having no purpose, and I do not mean a job. I mean a purpose to give my days direction and energy. I had a bit of a conversation with the leader, and then the discussion moved along.

Now, I had this burning question of purpose front and foremost in my mind. It is a question with which I struggle in prayer and meditation, and in therapy. While I was following the leader in her description of the obstacles, at some point, I mentally and spiritually "left" the retreat. I was still sitting at my table, and still had my notebook in front of me. My field of vision and attention narrowed to the pages of my notebook. I was transported to a place where I was able to hear the "sheer silence" of the Greatest Mystery.

What was offered me was that my thinking was all or nothing, that I was in search of one overarching purpose. I have myriad purposes, with one or more of them being my purpose at any given moment. This theophany was freeing! At long last, about two years in duration, I had a concept of my purpose that benefitted me. My spirit is at rest regarding the matter of purpose. My purpose is to be the me I am—a husband, father, grandfather, brother, sibling, friend, trumpet player, woodworker, published author, and . . .

The retreat leader had no idea of what was transpiring within me. To her, I simply looked like Bill at his table, writing in his journal. Nothing out of the ordinary there. I have not told her to this day about my experience. It was not just a retreat. It was an experience of something more.

It is possible that you have your own such moment. You find yourself standing at the watercooler, and your workmate's comment opens a new reality. You sense a message and reality much larger than the watercooler chitchat. You see new vistas open, you get an idea, and you behold promise and possibility heretofore unseen. Unless you tell the other person, they are oblivious to the reality that you are experiencing. They see themselves in that moment not as you see them. To them, they are simply chatting with you. To you, they are a portal to another realm.

The great teacher, Jesus of Nazareth, speaks directly to just such an experience. He was a man of prayer, and of spiritual retreat, frequently going away to meditate and reflect. One of his conversations is about doing deeds of compassion and kindness. He speaks to his disciples (students) of the naked, hungry, thirsty, stranger, and the prisoner (Matt 25:31–46). He simply and briefly describes the compassion extended to the naked by clothing them, to the hungry by feeding them, to the thirsty by giving them drink, to the stranger (alien) by welcoming them, and the prisoner by visiting them. There is nothing particularly new here. Then comes the eye-opener: "As you did it to the least of these, you did it to me."

The disciples are dismayed and confused by his comment. "What! How is that possible?" Jesus the Teacher is inviting the disciples to another realization, to one that sees more than meets the eye. He invites them to see him in the outcast, the marginalized, and the vulnerable—to discover in the interactions with these persons an opportunity to interact with him.

Awareness is a mystery. We know that we humans look for lost objects hiding in plain sight. We hunt for our lost glasses that are hanging around our neck or pushed up on our head. We turn the house upside down looking for our lost car keys, and the next morning find them glaring at us from the kitchen counter.

Mention has been made of a "thin veil," a slight separation between our world and the other world. A sheer gossamer screen overlays what is there in plain sight for those who have eyes that can see. Our experience of gazing at the ocean, the Grand Canyon, rainbow, or autumn tree discloses directly how our perceptions and awareness have their powers magnified in some common instances such that what is observed is not what is seen, and what is spoken, is not what is heard. More is seen. More is heard.

The thin veil that ordinarily shields our eyes from observing this "more," is by no means a heavy curtain. Wonder is all about us, for those who have eyes to see. Consider this comment: "Earth's crammed with heaven and every common bush afire with God, but only he who sees takes off his shoes. The rest sit around it, and pluck blackberries" (Elizabeth Barrett Browning, *From "Aurora Leigh"*).

The awe of the Greatest Mystery is that it seeks to touch us, to reach out to us, to relate to us, to you! The Greatest Mystery envelopes us, eliciting awe and wonder from us. The Greatest Mystery is present to us as that source of all. It communicates that we are unique, valued, esteemed, and loved, and that our individual life possesses meaning and purpose. This profound experience is one of being united with the Infinite, an experience of comm-union.

American religion in its Protestant Christian expressions builds primarily on the experience of the Greatest Mystery, not on arguments that prove the existence of God, i.e., the Greatest

Mystery. Sadly, this experience is framed by some in the Christian religious community as "conviction," meaning the human experiences him/herself as unworthy, a wretch who must confess his/her sins, and thrust themselves on the mercy of the Greatest Mystery. This framing of the Greatest Mystery as a convicting and condemning manifestation is largely indebted to Calvinism.

The emphasis on the holiness of the Greatest Mystery is used to bring center stage the lowliness of the individual. It is a moment of "I am not worthy." "I am inadequate." "What is someone like me doing in the presence of the Greatest Mystery?"

There is an alternative perspective and response to the frame of "conviction." This alternative response is one termed "affirmation." The experience of being touched by the Greatest Mystery provides the sense of worth that the Greatest Mystery is enveloping you. We experience the touch as one of affirmation. Being affirmed by the Greatest Mystery fills you with the stirring sense of being accepted. With the sense of affirmation, we are filled with joy. This perspective has none of the self-loathing, or self-deprecation that accompanies the perspective of conviction.

This alternative experience of the Greatest Mystery is one of accepting love. Certainly, the experience of the Greatest Mystery is an incomparable moment in which one is humbled by this instance of experiencing the Greatest Mystery. It is a moment when one's unimportance and smallness are present. Ironically, it is this same sense of unimportance, and of being undeserving of this experience, that dramatically highlight the grace and the love of this moment, a moment when the individual is affirmed, not convicted. The experience of the Greatest Mystery tangibly demonstrates the value and the inestimable worth of the individual; a moment of bliss and celebration, bordering on ecstasy. It is a moment of matchless joy.

Our experience of the Greatest Mystery is one of grace. It fills us with awe and wonder, as it is not a moment manufactured by human effort. By this experience, the Greatest Mystery bestows love and worth, freely pouring out both to all individuals.

That you were called into being and exist to this day are tangible signs that the Greatest Mystery loves you. From within the heart of the Greatest Mystery, you were called forth, shaped, and formed into the unique and individual being that is you. You are here because the Greatest Mystery wants you here, in this place, in this form, at this precise time. How marvelous for the Greatest Mystery to be so intentional about bringing you into being.

You possess distinct possibilities and creativities. How in touch are you with your sense of worth? Our sense of worth is foundational to our well-being. Do you consider yourself as adding to life with your humor, abilities, or courage? Do others tell you that you are a good listener, that you are dependable, or that you are good at your craft or profession? Being in touch with your capabilities and capacities, and hearing those recognized by others solidifies your sense of personal worth.

The greater our confidence in our worth, the greater our "self-esteem." We esteem that which is of significance. We want to like ourselves, to be proud of who we are, and to value ourselves. Most people esteem themselves, being fond of themselves, and discern themselves to be of worth. Some people do not esteem themselves. They have lost touch with their sense of worth, and do not like themselves. They judge themselves as having little to no worth. Being content is one indication that you know your worth and are in touch with it.

This affirmation and validation of your worth by the Greatest Mystery are not conditional. The affirmation and validation are for all eternity (no limits of time). The affirmation, worth, and validation are established, and in place apart from any expectations or requirements of behavior, or quality of heart and mind. Nothing we do, and nothing anyone or anything can do can separate us from this Love.

The Greatest Mystery is Love, whose nature it is to extend that Love. The Greatest Mystery is the gift-giver, and we are the gift-receiver. The Greatest Mystery is the ground of our knowledge that we are loved, that we matter, that our life has purpose and meaning.

What grace is bestowed upon us! All humans are touched by the Greatest Mystery, and have the experience of wonder and awe brought by this touch. Each of us responds to this touch at various times—some sooner, some later—and in alternate ways. While our response is unique with regard to time and manner, what we hold in common is the experience of the Greatest Mystery granting us eternal worth. It is an experience, an invitation, offered to all.

Given the genuineness and authenticity of the Greatest Mystery's touch, some may hold back their response out of fear. The person who has been hurt physically, emotionally, spiritually, or psychologically, understandably fears being hurt again—a risk they are reluctant to take, even in relationship to the Greatest Mystery.

Your fear of being hurt by the very ones saying that they value and love you sees you resorting to former means of self-protection from such betrayal and subsequent hurt. Hiding literally or figuratively, fleeing, closing the hatch on a storm shelter, or hunkering down in a protective shell are a means of being safe. These shelters can be trusted, and you have learned to rely on them to keep you unharmed. Telling you that you can trust the Greatest Mystery, and inviting you to come out of your hiding place, are words like what you have heard before. These reassurances are the lies you were previously told by those who ended up hurting you again. How do you move out of this fear?

The answer to this burning question has to do with the quality and the depth of the experience of the Greatest Mystery. This experience of worth, validation, love, and care is different in kind from previous experiences. This time, it is the ground of all, the Greatest Mystery enveloping you with affirmation and acknowledgment as a worthy and worthwhile person. The difference is the origin of the affirmation. The affirmation is not of human origin, but originates with the Greatest Mystery. This enveloping love asks nothing of you, and only gives acceptance to you, filling you with reassurance and trust.

Concurrently, the experience of the Greatest Mystery's communing with you is one of an unexperienced depth. The love and care are unfathomable, without limit and conditions. This experience is not superficial, or on the surface, of your life. No, its touch permeates and infuses you through and through, granting you a certainty and assurance new to you. We experience and know that we are worthwhile, worthy, and affirmed by that which has no name—the Greatest Mystery. We turn next to explore this affirming and validating love.

BOUNDLESS LOVE AND TOUCH

The affirming and validating love of the Greatest Mystery is boundless. Boundless Love is not a love limited to a certain amount, or quantity, which must be sipped sparingly to last a lifetime. There is no end to the availability of Boundless Love. It is abundant, abounding, and unending. It has an ever-enlarging horizon, expanding and expanding. It has no circumstances and no conditions. It is a clear spring, waiting for our cupped hands to lap it up. It is fresh, warm, and oven-cooked bread, waiting on the table to be tasted, enjoyed, and fill us with nutrition and nourishment. Are you thirsting for worthiness? Have a drink. Are you hungering to be deemed worthy? Have a bite. This water and bread are gifts for you!

One gift imparted by the touch of Boundless Love is the healing balm for a deep and persistent wound. This open wound, our root anxiety that we are lacking, and therefore need to take steps to prove and demonstrate our adequacy, if not superiority. Culture itself adds it voice to these internal denouncements, telling us we, indeed, are unworthy.

Judging ourselves to be inadequate, we look for ways to prove that we are adequate, and that we have worth. These are self-authenticating efforts, and require some outward accomplishment that "proves" that we are deserving, that we are worthy, and that we are good enough. These efforts are an "I will show you!" tactic to exhibit to the world that I am good enough. They are a maneuver to offer visible and tangible proof that we have worth.

These efforts put us first, and require a pride that can boast of its gains. Sadly, the accomplishments or demonstrations intended to prove to others and ourselves that we are worthy, only serve fleetingly to give us a sense of being good enough. Consequently, we must have more proof of our adequacy, and get to work to accumulate and achieve more outward signs and badges that show us and others how wonderful we are. The appetite of this hunger is bottomless and insatiable.

This cycle of inadequacy, proof of adequacy, the waning power of that proof, the re-appearance of our sense of inadequacy, and the quest of yet more proof, is unending. It is a runaway cycle.

Our efforts to stop this runaway cycle consist of a first-order change. The first-order change is one where we only need to try harder, and do more, and then—and only then—will we establish our sense of worthiness and adequacy for ourselves, and in the eyes of others. Such thinking generates a great deal of motion, but absolutely no movement! We are like squirrels in their spinning cage going around and around, running, while staying put! How do we escape this unsatisfying and exhausting cycle?

A second-order change is required for us to be freed from the flawed circular pattern of proving our worth. Boundless Love is the granted affirmation, not an acquired affirmation, that we are worthy and adequate. It is a pronouncement, and an ultimate acceptance of us as we are—warts and all. Our worth is stated as a new status, a new identity, as we are acclaimed as of worth, and as good enough—an accomplished status!

Boundless love, or "unconditional love," is concretely evidenced by your very being. You are here on earth, and not by your own powers. Ponder that sheer fact. You have life. You are being. Clearly the Greatest Mystery loves you, as the Greatest Mystery sorted all the innumerable possibilities and potentials to shape the you that is distinctly you.

You know that the very fact of your being means that the Greatest Mystery thinks that you are a promising idea, and so conceived you in its mind. Uniquely constituted and knit together in the Greatest Mystery's womb, and the womb of your mother, you were formed and shaped, and prepared for entry into this world. All of your being created is a work of love.

Now, you are being, you are life. How wonderful, is it not, that the hand of the Greatest Mystery lovingly molded your clay into the beautiful and wonder-full person you are! You are a creation of love, a creature into whom the life-giving Spirit of the Greatest Mystery is breathed Your being embodies unconditional love, a love so great it is incomprehensible, and beyond measure. This love is boundless. Hug yourself, embracing the love that is throughout you, that is you. You are loved, and are love, the Greatest Mystery's love, bearing the form of the distinct and unique you.

What is true about you, is true about every other human on this planet. Each one of them was designed, then formed, by the Greatest Mystery, who deemed all this individuality as a promising idea. That idea was shaped and knit in their mothers' wombs, and then birthed, sign and symbol of Holy Love resulting in a human. Their existence is a tangible sign of God's love for them, as it is for you.

It is incumbent upon all humanity to grant respect, dignity, and kindness to one another. No one person, no one nation, no one people, no one race or gender, is superior to another. Every human shares equally in the dignity of being a child of the Greatest Mystery, a creation of the Greatest Mystery, a being called forth in love. Amid this equality, there is distinctiveness and uniqueness, and no superiority, or "better than."

This unbounded love is not fettered, tethered, or limited by any constraint. It touches all with a free and generous abandon. This Love comes unbidden, and blows where it will. It brings sunshine. It brings nurturing. Both sunshine and rainfall freely shower on all. The sun shines on the just and the unjust. Rain falls on the unjust and the just. The sun's brightness can be seen by all. The sunlight brightens the day, bringing light and warmth to all. Rain's life-giving moisture can be smelled, seen, and felt by all. You do not need a ticket for either event!

This inclusive and grace-full love makes it possible for us to love ourselves, and others. Because we are loved by the Greatest Mystery, we in turn can love. When the Greatest Mystery imparts love, it also implants love! Love resides in us. It is generally recognized that humans love to the degree that they experience love.

That experience begins in utero. Parents play with the in utero fetus, patting and rubbing mom's tummy, or watching a foot or elbow traverse mom's abdomen. Parents play music for the fetus. They talk to the fetus. They read to the fetus. The immediate family and close friends join in with these activities. The fetus is known to sense these touches, hear the sounds of music, and of voices. The external environment of the fetus in utero is yet another component of its development.

Hopefully, these expressions of love continue at birth. Typically, the baby's birth is met with exclamations of joy. The newborn baby is placed on mom's chest for cuddling and cooing. This initial warm embrace by Mom, along with Dad and the broader family, are merely the beginning of a protracted process of the infant experiencing love.

Mental health professionals know full well that these initial and continuing expressions of love to the fetus, and the newborn infant, and through early infancy and childhood, are the foundations for developing a sense of trust, self, autonomy, belonging, and worthiness. These expressions cannot be taken for granted, and no one is guaranteed loving and nurturing parents. Those who are loved and wanted at birth are indeed blessed. The soil from which humility springs is this love and sense of blessing, and next we turn to consider humility as part of our experience of the Greatest Mystery.

HUMILITY AND TOUCH

Humility is the inescapable response when your experience of the Greatest Mystery affirms and validates that you are a unique being, called into life by that which imparts and implants boundless love in you. With worth bequeathed to you unconditionally, you can only be humbled. As a sign of your worth, you are gifted with vision in technicolor, hearing, taste, touch, loving, thinking, laughing, creating, and imagining. Your gift list grows longer, as it dawns on you that you also a recipient of the glories and wonders of civilization—art, electricity, music, medicine, religion, running and drinkable water, theatre, technology, communication, and language. Not to be outdone, nature itself stands in line to offer you gifts of air, water, soil, beauty, grandeur, majesty, power, comfort, and inspiration.

Such generosity boggles the mind, and takes away our breath. There is another gift, that of the presence of the Greatest Mystery within you. You are the dwelling place of the Greatest Mystery. The Greatest Mystery is in all, through all, and connected to all. You are the abode of the Sacred Presence. You are a child of the universe, a child of the Greatest Mystery, a part of the Greatest Mystery, while also apart from the Greatest Mystery. There is nothing required of you, nor are you capable of doing anything to earn, achieve or acquire your sacred status and reality. You are born that way, born as a child of the Greatest Mystery. That childhood comes directly and only from the Greatest Mystery. Humility is the result of this awareness.

It is one thing to acknowledge that the Greatest Mystery resides in us. It is quite another matter to comprehend that we dwell in the Greatest Mystery. In truth, the Greatest Mystery is our dwelling place. Given that the Greatest Mystery resides in us, and that we live and move and have our being in the Greatest Mystery, the term "abide" shows the mutuality between us and the Greatest Mystery. Earlier, I stated that the Greatest Mystery envelopes us, setting limits and holding open possibilities. The Greatest Mystery in whom we dwell then is our biosphere. We are not separate from the Greatest Mystery, nor is the Greatest Mystery separate from us. We and the Greatest Mystery are conjoined. The Greatest Mystery is your residence, your abode in which you live and move and have your being.

Our interior world and the exterior world, while distinct, yet overlap and are in communion with one another, united as dwellings for the Greatest Mystery. This unity makes it possible for the experience of the Greatest Mystery to come from within us, or to occur in external interactions with nature or humans.

The Greatest Mystery dwells among the people, as seen in the Jewish tabernacle and the *Shekinah*, and in the Christian Word (*Logos*) entering the world, and dwelling in the world. The tabernacle was the dwelling place for the *Shekinah* (Spirit of God), and where God was present (Exod 25:1–39). Christians saw the *Logos* (Word) dwelling in Jesus Christ, such that God's presence was experienced in this Jesus Christ. How amazing. How stunning. The Greatest Mystery is both transcendent, and yet immanent, dwelling among us, and being present to us.

Our humility grants other people some space, and gives them slack. We can ease up on them because we ease up on ourselves. We know that we have the Greatest Mystery's boundless love that affirms and validates us, "warts and all." We are not perfect, but we are loved! People are generally doing the best they can with the experience and knowledge that is presently theirs. Do we not want others to think so of us?

Jesus offered several teachings on humility. His teaching about the speck in our neighbor's eye, and the plank in our eye is well-known (Matt 7:1–5) It is the dearth of humility that enables a person with a plank protruding from his/her eye, to be able to discern a speck in the neighbor's eye. A humble person realizes that he/she has enough shortcomings and challenges to occupy all their energy and effort.

The basis of our humility is twofold: we have life; we are unique. When it dawns on us that we were given the gift of life by the Greatest Mystery, we are humbled. We were called into being, and not by our own doing. In other terms, we are the "creature," and not the "Creator." Remembering our true identity will help ward off our pomposity and vanity.

We also are unique. There has never been another "you," nor will there be another "you." What distinguishes you, and makes you unique are gifts. The gifts of your physical appearance, nationality, race, emotional makeup, mental abilities, creativity, and physical abilities are not of your doing. All that sets you apart has been given to you. You are a steward of these gifts, a cultivator, not the creator.

So it is that humility leads to gratitude. Knowing the Greatest Mystery's boundless love calls us into being, affirms us, grants us unique gifts, and causes a deep sense of gratitude to well up inside us. We turn next to gratitude as part of the experience of the Greatest Mystery.

GRATITUDE AND TOUCH

Each morning begins with a gift. It is important that we stay in touch with the truth that the day to which we are awakened is the only day we have, and the day in its entirety is not a sure thing. What we do know is that the new day is the first day of the rest of our life. Additionally, we live with the comprehension that this new day may well be the last day of our life. Such a gift of a day of life is an expression of love, a gift for which gratitude is the spontaneous outburst. This day, and our being alive, are not products of our own hand. No, our life, and this day, are handed to us as a gift, tied with a bow.

Gratitude has the power to open our eyes to tidbits of joy throughout the day, and the power to bring a smile to our face even though . . . Some of these tidbits are the gifts of our bodies, minds, spirits, and your life itself. Are you in touch with the marvel of your body, and how it does its best to serve you?

You have the gift of creativity, which you display at work, home, and among friends. Creativity is not the sole property of those who compose symphonies or paint a masterpiece. All of us are artists and creators. The way you perform your job and fulfill your responsibilities is unique to you. You put your own imprint on it. How you phrase your sentences, greet your spouse or partner, hug your grandchildren are all artistically crafted by you. Your loved ones know your signature facial expressions, body language, and phrases. The way you decorate your shop, cubicle, office, or home are creative expressions. If you have hobbies or interests, that is your creativity expressing itself. Stay in touch with your creativity, for it brings you energy.

Friends are a gift. They offer you affirmation, love, and support. People whom we count as friends freely choose to gift us with their friendship, an occasion for gratitude. Stay in touch with the reality that there is no "I have to" in friendship, only "I want to." Friends are not to be taken for granted. Each day of friendship offered to you is a gift, one that fills you with joy.

Nature is a gift-given, and a gift-giver. Nature possesses unequalled power to reunite you with your gratitude. Do you think it odd that nature gifts us, and in doing so, elicits joy and gratitude in us? Stay in touch with the fact that the planet predates you, and from your birth forward, spreads before you all the treasures it has to offer. You find gratitude in the majestic grandeur, and the moving encouragement of nature with its many faces and expressions of power, beauty, and intricacy. Nature gifts us with peace, comfort, strength, awe, and inspiration. Mother nature has many remedies and medicines for our human maladies, and all are free for the asking. We are wise to stay in touch with Mother Nature, who so deeply cares for and delights in us.

Our experience of the Greatest Mystery energizes our gratefulness, and empowers us to restore our touch, with gratitude. We pass along gratitude to the people with whom we come in contact. Gratitude is both how we feel and how we interact with others. It cannot be contained or bottled up in us, as gratitude is communicable. It does your soul good, and it does good for the souls of those whom you meet during the day.

Thankfully, gratitude is communicable, and is spread by our exchanges with others. Indeed, our gratitude may prove to be just the antidote to another person's discontent. I am aware of the presence of ingratitude, and am of the mind that it lacks the power to withstand the ingratiating power of gratitude. With our gratitude for a new day of life, our friends, and the manifold gifts of Mother Nature, we bless and enhance the lives of those we encounter. The gratitude and joy in our hearts fills the space around us, and blesses the lives of others. The importance then of staying in touch with our gratitude is twofold: it immunizes us against discontent; it benefits those in our relationship circles.

To state that we need to stay in touch with our wonder and awe, boundless love, humility, and gratitude implies responsibility. Indeed, once we and the Greatest Mystery have extended our hands to one another, and gotten in touch, we have a responsibility from that point forward. Our conversation transitions to discuss that responsibility.

RESPONSIBILITY AND TOUCH

Boundless Love holds us accountable for how we fulfill our responsibilities. Love that does not contain accountability is something other than love. The absence of accountability really is the absence of care: "I don't care what you do." Or, the absence of accountability is a way of saying, "You do not matter to me—what you say, what you do, who you are, all are of no consequence to me!" That we have lost touch with our sense of responsibility is seen by our acting as if our words and deeds are without consequence. We behave with little or no regard for the consequences our words and deeds have for others. For as long as our words and deeds seemingly bring no consequences to us, we are fine with saying or doing whatever we wish. Boundless Love does not support this practice.

Boundless Love freely grants us affirmation, and affection. We are loved, accepted, and valued. These gifts evoke humility, gratitude, and a sense of responsibility. This responsibility takes the form of stewardship. The Greatest Mystery holds us accountable for how well we cultivate and nourish our own lives and being. We are held accountable for, and have a responsibility for, our relationships with others, the planet, and the Greatest Mystery.

Boundless Love holds us accountable for what is best mutually for our relationships, and for the well-being of the planet. Our accountability and responsibility are mutual: what is good and beneficial for all.

The accountability of our stewardship manifests itself in consequences and outcomes, those intended and those unintended. Our thoughts and deeds bear fruit. Some fruit we cultivate purposely and carefully, and other fruit appears as unexpected and unintended. The fruit of our hand is measured by the ruler of flourishing. Do our words and deeds create and sustain flourishing and well-being for ourselves, others, and Mother Nature? This ruler is the ethical standard by which words, actions, and plans are measured.

The opposite of flourish is wither. The Greatest Mystery's penchant for flourishing is easily visible in nature itself. Consider all the colors and hues in nature. Look at the myriad number of felines, fish, fowl, and foliage. Ponder people—so many assorted sizes, shapes, facial features, skin tone, height, stature, languages, and attire. Clearly the Greatest Mystery likes to see life flourish. Consequently, we are held accountable for the degree we facilitate and enhance flourishing. Conversely, to the degree that we are responsible for the presence of the powers of withering of others or the planet, we are also accountable.

Recall Elijah. He was held accountable and responsible by the Greatest Mystery. Elijah was given a responsibility to speak truth to power (the king), and to the people who were being misled by the policies of the queen. Summoned by the Greatest Mystery from the cave where he was hiding in fear, he comes forth to be accountable to the One who gave him a mission. He weathered a rock-splitting wind, a ground-shaking earthquake, and an earth-scorching fire. Then he was face to face with "sheer silence." Others may have turned and run from the wind, earthquake, and fire. Some may have found the "sheer silence" deadening, if not maddening. Perhaps Elijah's knees did tremble a bit. We do not know that. We do know that the Greatest Mystery promised Elijah help, which rejuvenated Elijah, and put him back in motion (1 Kgs 19:9–18). There is often a revitalizing dimension of being held accountable.

It took quite some measure of courage for Elijah to subject himself to being held accountable. It took courage for Elijah to stand in the mouth of the cave before the wind, earthquake, fire, and sheer silence. We do know that he was courageous enough to stay the course, and respond to the Greatest Mystery's revelation. Now we move forward to examine the courage required of us.

COURAGE AND TOUCH

Our experience of the Greatest Mystery puts us in touch with Boundless Love. You sense the affirmation and acknowledgment of your worth. Your name is engraved upon the palms of the Greatest Mystery. These hands hold you, protect you, guide you, and present possibilities beyond count. The hairs on your head are numbered as the Greatest Mystery combs, brushes, and braids your hair. There is no greater source of care, protection, safety, and love than that of the Greatest Mystery. You are secure, and you trust completely the Greatest Mystery with your well-being.

Secure and anchored in trust of the Greatest Mystery, it is possible for you to live courageously and creatively. Living takes courage. It requires courage to call forth the unique gifts implanted in us by the Greatest Mystery, and to be accountable for our stewardship of those gifts.

Courage is not the absence of fear. Courage recognizes, and acknowledges fear. Courage possesses the mettle to extend a welcome to fear. Courage acknowledges fear's existence and presence. Fear is shown respect, and is honored as a reality. A courageous person acknowledges fear. A fool does not know enough to be afraid.

Sadly, for our nation, and our world, a sizeable number of people have lost touch with their courage, leaving fear free to roam and pillage the land, igniting fires of division and fragmentation. Society is in a frenzy of fear, a frenzy easily fed by unchecked and uninspected rumors and outright lies.

There is the fear in several corners that the world of the whites, and of white males particularly, is threatened by people of color. This demise of white power and privilege "must be avoided at all costs," shouts the fear. There is dread that women will be in positions of equity and power, filling some men with trepidation. Fear takes over the minds and hearts of people who are afraid of those individuals whose sexual orientation and identity is not determined by their genitals.

Fingers tighten around pistol grips, stocks of rifles, and the triggers of automatic weapons capable of mass killings. This gun-clutching is fueled by the NRA, and the multiple parties of a peculiar interpretation of the Second Amendment. The peculiar interpretation holds that it is a gun owner's "right" to own not sporting guns, but slaughter weapons and weapons of the battlefield.

The "1 percenters" fear the 99 percent who want health insurance, livable wages, full-time employment at one job rather than multiple part-time jobs, clean air and water, good schools, a robust infrastructure, and dignity. The fear is the 99 percenters will somehow take away the 1 percenters' wealth and status.

Polluting industries and corporations fear environmental concerns. The fear is that environmental concerns will put ecology above economics. In truth, ecology and good economics are more compatible than competitive. Such is the power of fear that it blinds people to economic good sense. Across our nation, we behold people lacking courage, and living in fear, a situation shockingly ironical in the "home of the brave."

Courage dares to hope. Hope takes a valiant stand against fear. Hope is not blind, naïve, or dumb about the present or the future. Authentic hope has the power to read the situation, and take an accurate account of its limits and possibilities. Doing so, hope clings bravely to what is unseen, yet will be manifested.

Hope is courageously realistic, not a delusion or a fantasy. Hope's sunlight evaporates the mists and vapors of fear, an ephemeral beast at best. Like the little boy who shouted that "the king has no clothes," hope valiantly speaks truth to fear, which flees back to the dark from whence it was beckoned. Hope has the strength of titanium and the power of a laser to forge a beneficial present and light the way forward to a promise-filled future.

Getting back in touch with the courage instilled by the experience of the Greatest Mystery's Boundless Love, allows us to live freely, abundantly, and securely. We need gun owners of courage who can advocate for guns to be owned for sport and self-defense, and not for assault and mass murder. We need 1 percenters who are courageous enough to create a tax system where they pay their fair share of taxes, and where good-paying jobs abound to build and sustain a flourishing national economy, while being ecologically compatible. We need courageous corporate leaders who can lead the way in leaving behind dinosaur-age fossil-fueled power production, and who can be innovators in clean and renewable energy sources for transportation, power, and production.

Only by restoring touch with our courage are we able to embody the Golden Rule. "Do unto others as you would have them do to you" (Matt 7:12 NRSV). It requires courage to internalize and live the Two Great Commandments. "You shall love the LORD your God with all you heart, soul, and mind. You shall love your neighbor as yourself" (Matt 22:37–39 NRSV).

Restoring touch with our courage gives us the valor to look at truth, listen to the studied and seasoned reasoning of science, and stare without blinking at the ecological disaster awaiting us, unless we muster the bravery to take prompt and decisive action. Courage gives us the spine to listen to the sociologists, wise politicians, and scholars who are sounding the alarms about the disaster our democracy faces unless our society, judicial, and political systems are restored. The fearful are unable to face the truth. Ho, people of fear, your courage is needed now! "If not now, when? If not you, who?"

Your courage is vital for your well-being. It takes courage to accept the Boundless Love offered by the Greatest Mystery. Boundless Love can be dismissed or brushed aside, both indicative of fear. Courage says "thank you" to the Greatest Mystery for the gift of Boundless Love. Boundless Love establishes your worth, a worth that is granted, not somehow earned. It is a worth that is eternal, assuring unconditionally that you are held in esteem, that your worth is permanent.

It takes courage to accept the worth granted by Boundless Love, as now you are responsible to be the person you were created to be. Energized by your courage, you are an artist of your life, creating novelty with the gifts of creativity that are uniquely yours. You can follow your purpose, and craft a structure of meaning.

You can enjoy the wonder and awe present in life, and live grate-fully, and humbly. Give your hand and heart to courage, and find joy and fulfillment.

The image of the artist crafting, fashioning, and shaping his or her life into a creative splendor points to the sense of mean-ing and fulfillment that is available to those who have accepted the Greatest Mystery's extended hand. Our dialogue takes us to an examination of a fulfilled life.

FULFILLMENT AND TOUCH

Integral to the experience of the Greatest Mystery is the aware-ness that the Greatest Mystery intends for us to live a fulfilled and fulfilling life. The Greatest Mystery that wants us here on earth, and delights in our being, intends that we be happy. To be happy is to live a fulfilling life. Happiness is not purchasing the newest electronic device for a bargain-basement price. True happiness is much more profound, and much deeper. When you sense that the life you are living fulfills you, that is happiness! When you lose touch with what brings you fulfillment, then you lose happiness.

Blessed is a richer word for happy. Jesus' Beatitudes is a teach-ing about life's profound blessings, the blessings of comfort, jus-tice, mercy, dignity, redemption, recognition, and the presence of God (Matt 5–7). Such blessings demark a fulfilled life, one where we sense that we matter to the Greatest Mystery.

This quest for a blessed life, a fulfilled life, is by no means an ego trip. It is not a selfish pursuit. It is not narcissistic. The quest for a fulfilled life is to accomplish the Greatest Mystery's intentions for you. Your life task is to pay homage to your unique gifts and quali-ties, to be who were created to be. The Greatest Mystery made you a one-of-a-kind human. You cannot be replicated or duplicated. No amount of DNA rescripting will make another "You." Such a duplicate cannot have the same parents, be born at the same time on the same day and year, experience the same ebb and flow of pol-itics and history, know the identical fluctuations of the economy, be saddened by the same acts of war and violence, and so on, with all the person-forming factors of consciousness and context. It is time for you to get back in touch with the Greatest Mystery's wish for you to be happy, to express your uniqueness, and to be fulfilled.

Accompanying this treasure and these gifts of creativity is the energy to empower and actualize the flourishing of them. You were placed here not to cower before others, and bow down to them and their expectations. No, your purpose is to flourish and prosper, to live fully a fulfilling life crafted by you, a piece of art from your own creative hand. You are not a candle to be hidden, but a fire to be ignited. Get in touch with that.

It requires courage and curiosity to examine and critique the expectations that society wants to place upon our shoulders as a yoke. Our families have expectations of "what people in our family do." Our parents have expectations of "what a child of mine/ours will do." Society and culture both have expectations of what makes for a successful and acceptable life.

Your authentic goal is to be fulfilled and fulfilling. Chasing after the expectations of others to be deemed successful is truly a dog chasing its tail. Pursuing a fulfilling life is one with direction and purpose, one guided by you.

Living a life that is fulfilling requires you to stay focused, and determined. Well-meaning people may tell you that you are wasting your life pursuing what offers you fulfillment. Maybe you want to paint in oil, while your family wants you to join the ranks of the family business. Maybe you want to play in a rock band, and not practice dentistry, or be a researcher or academic in astrophysics. The pressure can be enormous in these instances. You may waver. You may be tempted to "try it for a bit." You may doubt yourself. When such thoughts and feelings descend upon you, your escape is the path of fulfillment.

Ask yourself in your wondering, "What do I want? What fulfills me?" These questions will help you right your ship. They will be the compass points helping you to get back on course. They will put you back in touch with the fulfilled life that matters greatly to you.

We are at an intersection. We leave the topic of the *spiritual* self, and turn to the topic of the *deepest* self. Our focus is getting in touch with our deepest self, and to that endeavor we now turn.

OUR DEEPEST SELF AND TOUCH

We all on occasion find that we are out of touch with ourselves. Beyond these periodic instances of getting out of touch with ourselves, we may find ourselves in a season where we lose touch with our deepest self. This season may be elongated such that we reach a point where we do not recognize ourselves anymore. These moments can be frightening, anxiety-producing, or disheartening. Over time, we realize that the person that we were is gone. Concurrently, we discover that we are out of touch with the person we have now become. "Who am I, anyway?" This question points to our loss of touch with our deepest self. Our deepest self, or soul, is the residence for our identity, purpose, and meaning.

It requires honesty and courage to ask, "Who am I, anyway?" An additional dose of courage and honesty is required to provide an answer to the question, an honest answer! The question is not "Who do I want to be?" or "Who was I?" or "Who should I be?" These questions are not about reality, but about wishes. The question "Who am I?" is about the present, about who you are in the now, at this very moment. The initial step in restoring touch with the deepest self is an authentic analysis and answer to this basic question.

In contrast to the gradual loss of touch with our deepest self, disruptive and traumatic events instantly put us out of touch with our deepest self. Being out of touch begins with the numbing shock of a jarring event. Depending on how willing we are to be in touch with the thoughts and feelings generated by the jarring event, we correspondingly influence the degree to which we are in touch with our deepest self.

What is going on when we ask, "Who is the real me?" It is a question attempting to get us back in touch with our deepest self after a world-altering trauma. This question is poignantly raised by trauma and tragedy itself. It is a question also raised by how effectively our coping mechanisms and resources allow us to stay in touch with the thoughts and feelings surrounding the trauma.

My own ineffective efforts illustrate this point. Years ago, I was burned over 23 percent of my body in a propane fire. Our two daughters were out of harm's way. My wife got burns on her hands from beating out the flames, and her hair was singed from bending over me in those efforts.

My inability to accept the reality of what happened to me began when my flames were out, and I asked my wife, "How do I look?" "Fine," she replied. I did not look fine. My shirt was burned almost completely off, and my beard had been removed by the flames. My hands and forearms had third-degree burns. I was clueless.

I continued to be clueless as I attempted to turn on the back-yard hose. I intended to extinguish the burning material the propane had ignited, fearing that the house might catch fire. I tried to turn the faucet handle, and felt my hands slip and slide. I looked at my hands. They were as big as hot dogs that had been overcooked, and split open. I was unable to accept my serious state. Denial was hard at work.

An ambulance arrived, and the paramedics quickly cut off the remainder of my shirt and jeans in the driveway. I was surrounded by neighbors and friends, and our friend directly across the street held my head in her lap. The ambulance crew administered morphine, which is when the pain stopped. The ambulance transported me to a burn unit in Los Angeles, California, at the Daniel Freeman Hospital, where I would spend a month.

Shortly after I arrived in the burn unit, the plastic surgeon came to see me. I asked him to bandage me up, as I had to drive my family to Kansas the next day, where I had a new job. He looked at me and said, "You will be here at least a month." That moment is when the depression hit me. I knew without a doubt that I was seriously injured, and needed the care of a burn unit.

During my stay, I was tubbed twice a day, morning and afternoon. Being "tubbed" means undergoing debriding, where a sponge is used to scrape away dead and dying skin. When the debriding was judged to have done its work, I had one surgery, receiving skin grafts on my hands, forearms, and hip pointers. My thighs were the donor sites for the skin required to fashion these grafts. I did not require surgery on my face, nose, and ears, for which I am grateful. I wore Jobst garments (pressure garments on my thighs, hands, and arms) for a year following the accident. The purpose of these garments is to reduce scarring, and in my case, they were highly effective.

During my hospitalization, my main thought was to get to my new job as the senior minister of the Park Place Christian Church (Disciples of Christ), Hutchinson, Kansas. I spent little, if any, time processing what happened to me, and what could have happened to my wife and our two children. I had intrusive, invasive, and recurring memories of the sights and sounds of the fire. No one on the hospital staff—nurse, chaplain, social worker—was available to guide and help me process my experience.

I continue to have triggers that make me vigilant (forty years later). I am wary of our gas grill (propane), and make sure it is turned off after every use. The "whoosh" sound of the grill igniting makes me uneasy. Movies that show people in fire, or people on fire, are difficult for me. Sometimes I close my eyes.

My treatment for depression continues, which includes medications and therapy. I had my first anxiety attack weeks after arriving in Hutchinson. I did see a physician after that episode, who told me that I had an anxiety attack—no follow-up visits or treatment were prescribed. I know now that anxiety and depression frequently appear together.

I finally got into treatment for depression years later when I was diagnosed with prostate cancer, which was treated surgically. This time, with the threat posed by the prostate cancer, I took seriously the threat while keeping a positive outlook. I believe that I am doing a better job today at staying in touch with my deepest self than was the case when I was burned.

Trauma is not the only cause for us to be out of touch with our deepest self. Our coping mechanisms can gloss over intense thoughts and feelings, putting us out of touch with our deepest self. The way we respond or attempt to cope with the crisis can itself put us out of touch with our deepest self.

Even everyday experiences prompt us to wonder if we are in touch with our deepest self. For instance, we may be jolted by events at work or home that lead us to ask, "When did I lose touch with my marriage, or my job?" We query ourselves, "How did I get so out of touch?" These situations and similar ones are generally managed by acknowledging the problem, and discussing resolutions. Avoiding the process of acknowledgment and resolution puts us further out of touch with our deepest self, and imperils our relationships at home and work.

Addictions are one way we attempt to cope with losing touch with our deepest self. Screens are a new fact of life, and a new addiction. Screen time is inevitable, as screens are present at the grocery store, the ATM, schools, work, vehicle, home, the airport, TVs, computers, and handheld devices. The question is not, will you spend time looking at a screen, but how much time will you give to the screen?

Screen time is not without consequences. Some studies recommend a daily limit of two hours of screen time for children and youth ages three to eighteen years old. Other studies have found a connection between screen time and childhood obesity, interrupted sleep patterns, and social and behavioral problems. These findings are not interested in putting screens in a bad light. The findings point to the need for parents to exercise control over the amount of time their children spend with screens.

Adults spend quite a bit of time on screens themselves, up to eleven hours a day. While work today routinely involves the use of a computer screen, it is the at-home and after-work screen time that puts adults out of touch with their deepest self. A screen can be numbing. When an individual is looking at her/his screen, that person is not present. The claim "I am listening to you," while texting, is not true. Attention requires focus, and the screen wins in these situations.

At home, adults have their screens out at the dinner table, and while watching a TV program or movie. Again, the person with the screen in their hand, is not present to others.

Gaming is an excellent example of how screens are a gateway to another realm. While gaming, the person takes on an alter ego, and an alter identity, living in another world, one of make-believe and fantasy. It is common for gamers to stay up late at night, unable to go to sleep as they are so enthralled in their game. One study points out that games give players a shot of dopamine when they "win" or triumph over an opponent. Dopamine is called "candy for the brain." Games turn on the centers of the brain related to cravings like those for drugs and gambling. It is this dopamine that makes gaming addictive, and a hard habit to break. Screens have a tremendous power to sever touch with our deepest self.

Submerging ourselves into the altered state of consciousness arrived at with substances of various sorts, only wreaks havoc on our lives, and destroys our health. The drug of choice in our society is alcohol. It is a legal substance, and socially acceptable.

We are seeing the dawning of a new drug of choice, marijuana. Although federal law makes the possession and sale of marijuana illegal, states across the nation are legalizing the sale and possession of it. Many states now have retail outlets for recreational marijuana, and for medical marijuana.

Medical marijuana has recognized healing and therapeutic powers, and is available only with a physician's prescription. It is a positive option for people experiencing chronic and acute pain. In contrast to the health benefits of medical marijuana, both legal and illegal substances are forms of self-medication used to alter our consciousness. This altered consciousness creates an unreal world, and provides an escape hatch from the realities of life. Seeking escape is a sign of how discontented we are with our lives, and the presence of a painful emptiness within us.

An obsession with, an addiction to, or a dependence upon the altered consciousness provided by the misuse of alcohol, and illicit and illegal drugs, is a danger to our health, our relationships, and our careers and employment. The daily ingestion of toxic amounts of alcohol overworks, and eventually kills our liver. This condition is known as cirrhosis of the liver. We need a healthy liver to stay alive.

Excessive amounts of alcohol, and other drugs, also affect our brain, and thus our cognitive abilities. We no longer are rational and reasonable, and become adept at denying that we have a problem, and that our alcohol consumption is causing problems at home and work. The alcohol affects our thinking to such an extent that a fantasy (inebriated) world is now the world we inhabit.

We are such a humorous society inasmuch as we are prudish about sex—premarital sex is frowned on, pornography can only be purchased from "Adult Video" stores (who has a video player anymore?)—while at the same time our culture highlights sex and sexiness. We buy pornography off the internet. Going to an "Adult" store for porn is so last century. Our TV shows and movies are replete with "soft porn," and sometimes quite explicit sex acts.

A new addiction has been identified: "sex addiction." This new addiction does not possess clinical credentials, as shown by not being listed in the *Diagnostic and Statistical Manual 5* (*DSM-5*). Even so, our society's preoccupation with sex shows our need for excitement and stimulation to mask our empty state.

Prodigious and prolific sexual activity and prowess fail to abate our emptiness. Many men spend their screen time on pornography sites, where they find worth in imagining they are capable of unrealistically arousing women (or men). Men pursue pornography on the internet while at work, using the company computer as much as possible. These men are not merely discontent with their sexual life, there is a missing core contentment that elects to display itself as a sexual hungering and seeking, which if met, will lead to contentment. This preoccupation by men will weary their partners, and leave men empty-handed, exhausted, and discontent.

We live in a society addicted to stuff (possessions). Acquiring stuff and more stuff somehow is supposed to signal our worth. The advertising world is practiced at coming up with new stuff that we "have to have." Our landfills are bulging to overflowing with our discarded stuff. We rent storage space to house the stuff for which we do not have room in our homes and garages. We are drowning in a sea of stuff, and continue to turn the faucet handle open further to flood our lives with more stuff. The thought is that eventually we will have just the right stuff, and will no longer feel empty.

Usually a crisis of some sort, called "hitting the bottom," is required to usher reality into our lives. Reality is determined, and will not be shown the door as it has business to conduct. It focuses its laser beam on the havoc at home, chaos at work, the demolition of personal health, and the mayhem strewn around the swath cut by your addiction(s). Reality may come as an intervention by caring friends, who are worried at your self-destructive behavior. Perhaps a group of coworkers will band together to approach you in hope that you will seek professional help. Your family, spouse, and children may engage you to describe accurately the swath of pain and chaos, event by event, which lies in your wake. Your family will pledge their love and support as a way of encouraging and supporting you to get help.

Gazing at what you have wreaked, you are only able to ask, "How did I lose touch with myself, my thoughts, feelings, behaviors?" "What happened to me?" "Who have I become?" "What am I doing to my life?" "What am I doing to the lives of those who care about me?" "How did I lose touch with the health of my body, mind, spirit?" These questions signal an awareness of lost touch with your deepest self, and hold open the potentiality of taking steps to get back in touch with it.

THE DEEPEST SELF IS EMBODIED

Human life is an embodied experience. Our body is not distinct from us, nor is embodied life optional. Our body is how we exist, how we interact, and how we experience life. It is crucial that we stay in touch with being embodied. Embodied is how humans do life.

The Middle Eastern religions of Judaism, Islam, and Christianity see human bodily existence as one established by God. After creating humans, God is quoted as saying, "It is very good" (Gen 1:31). We are embodied beings from the instant of our creation, and the embodied state is pronounced as "good!"

Artificial intelligence, production-line robots, and humanlike robots are expressions of our fascination with the human brain. Clearly, these electronic innovations can outperform humans at many levels. Robotic surgery devices, guided by human eyes and hands, can perform intricate and precise ophthalmological procedures. Human strength and speed are magnified by equipment worn to enhance battlefield capabilities. Supercomputers can perform computations at a speed and magnitude beyond human ability. Multiple home electronic assistants control appliances, operate home security systems, and do research on questions ranging from "What is the current temperature?" to "Who were the signers of the Declaration of Independence?"

None of the above functions are human thinking. These activities are computations, a machine executing complicated algorithms. Human thinking occurs in an organ, floating in cerebral fluid, encased in a cranium, dependent on O_2 and nourishment delivered by a circulatory system of blood. Human thinking entails emotions, thoughts, and the life history of the individual. It is a process that factors in the current circumstances, as well as hoped for outcomes and consequences.

It is beneficial for us to acknowledge that feelings are also a galaxy of embodied entities working cooperatively. Neuropsychology is learning more about how particular areas of the brain are involved in certain emotions, as clinicians also are broadening their knowledge of the various hormones and their role in feelings. We know feelings affect various parts of the body, with stress manifesting itself in tight shoulder muscles, facial and skull muscles, and our abdomen. Stress also can be detected in elevated blood pressure, elevated heart rate, and elevated respiratory rate. Feeling is more than an emotion. It is an array.

HUMANS ARE ANIMALS

It is important to stay in touch with a basic fact: we are mammals. As a member of the animal kingdom, we are one of multiple mammals. *Homo* is our genus, and *sapiens* is our species. We *sapiens* are the only non-extinct species of the genus *Homo*. Among the mammals, we are one of numerous primates. We possess many common features shared among primates. Yet, we are endowed with unique features, such as the size of our brain, and the range of motion of our opposing thumb. Human babies are helpless at birth, and continue to be dependent and vulnerable for a protracted period, distinguishing us from other mammals and primates, whose young are more independent at an earlier age than human young.

The Genesis account of creation underscores the kinship of humans and animals, for they both receive the Spirit of God, "the breath of life." In this account, the religious and spiritual traditions of Judaism and Christianity hold in common that both animals and humans are embodied beings. Both beings are creatures of flesh, and both receive and contain the animating breath of God.

God's Spirit, or breath, is the creating power of the Greatest Mystery that moves over the formless deep, calling forth order to replace the chaos. For Judaism and Christianity alike, God's breath, or Spirit, is the creating, ordering, sustaining, renewing, and novelty-establishing power of all reality (Gen 1:1ff. NRSV). It is this cosmos-creating power that is breathed into humans and animals, a kinship with which we need to stay in touch.

Animals live in our world, and in their own inner world. They are smart. Ask a scientist about the intelligence of a pig or a dolphin. They have vocal expression and a unique language, and communicate, both verbally and nonverbally.

Animals are not dumb, as in lacking the ability to think, or the ability to communicate. They can problem-solve, and send and receive messages. They play. They have personalities. They are social. They are affectionate to us, and know us, and the vehicles we drive. They are loyal, and compassionate, sensitive to our moods. These and other traits serve to urge us to honor that we are mammals, holding much in common with animals.

The essential common feature of humans and animals is that our interiors house God's breath. God's breath resides, or dwells, within both human and animal. God's Spirit is not a foreign ingredient, or an ingredient mixed in at a later point in a human's and animal's life, but an essential component of human and animal life from the beginning. The Greatest Mystery is an indwelling presence, as well as a presence experienced in nature.

Staying in touch with the fact that we are mammals allows us to respect a basic fact: we are one with all creation. We are not apart, or better. While we are distinctive among primates and mammals, we must respect our kindred animals. We are not distinct from the animal kingdom, but are members of that life class. We are considered to be the most intelligent of all mammals, even though other mammals have larger brains.

Our tendency is to view all creation from our perspective, one that is anthropocentric. This view has the world orbiting around humankind, making us the center of the universe. It is truer that we exist as a part of creation, not apart from creation. Consider how we are made. We are Spirit-animated, and constituted of dirt and water. Spirit, earth, water are our basic elements, and those of animals as well. This planet is the dust of the stars, which is fairly basic material, and humble in terms of building material. We call our planet of soil and water "Mother Earth." With that name, we pay homage to the womb of our origin. Since Earth is our Mother, is it any surprise that our physical composition reflects that of our parent?

THE DEEPEST SELF AND GENDER

Being in touch with our deepest self as embodied creatures who are mammals includes honoring our gender. Today, we realize that humans in their assigned birth gender, based on their genitals, may not match their internal gender, nor their gender expression. Gender is not either/or, this or that, but more of a spectrum. The intersex person is born with two sets of genitals, showing the complexity of gender. Gender is distinct from our genitals, and some of us with female genitals discover that we are male by internal gender. Others with male genitals learn that they are female by internal gender. Thankfully, in today's world of medicine, prescriptions and procedures are in place to help persons achieve their gender match and identity.

I realize that gender is now seen as being more of a continuum, rather than polar opposites. It is becoming more the case that individuals are asked to identify where they see themselves on that continuum. Most of us are cisgender individuals, meaning that our genitals and our internal gender align.

Gender features—brain structure, brain function, hormones, genes, physiology, senses, socialization—all influence how genders experience the world. These gender-specific qualities enable the genders to share common abilities, possess unique aspects, and lack powers and abilities found in the other genders. An illustration of gender differences is that the female brain matures more quickly than the male brain. Usually a female's brain matures at age twenty-one, and a male's brain is fully developed at age twenty-five. There is a difference between a testosterone-fed brain, and an estrogen-nourished brain.

These differences in perception and experience are simply that—different. The differences are not better, with one preferred over the other, or one less reliable than the other. Genders see the world differently, not rightly or wrongly, not better or worse.

Sadly, a woman's world is all too often one where they are viewed as prey, a world spotlighted by the #MeToo movement. This world treats women as objects subject to a man's predatory behavior. Rather than being appreciated for their skills and intellect, women inhabit a world where their abilities are dwarfed by their appearance. Women's ability to bear children may put their career and job at risk. While maternity leave is widespread, too many employed females find there are monetary, career, and position consequences surrounding pregnancy and birth.

Men need to get in touch with the biases and prejudices that depersonalize women. This effort requires asking how they as a man contribute to the presence and persistence of this world, asking what action they can take to change such a destructive world.

If you are wondering how you can get in touch with the world of a woman, here are two steps. One, ask one of the women who are important in your life to talk to you about their world. As they describe their world, your job is specific. That job is to listen. That is it. Listen. The second step is to engage yourself in self-reflection. Drawing upon what you learn from listening to a woman you value describe her world, ask yourself, "How do I participate in the building and maintaining of that world?" Be truthful and honest in this self-assessment. Next, ask yourself how you can change your speech and conduct to create a better world. Consider who among your male friends you can enlist to confront and change the current world of women.

Males live in a world shaped and influenced by genes, hormones, physiology, and society. Society generally grants men a wide array of interests and pursuits—ballet dancers, martial arts fighters, engineers, schoolteachers, carpenters, artists, nurse, writers, or truck drivers. Whatever life path a man may take, from the military to the ministry, he may find moments when certain expectations surface. These constricting expectations are: men don't cry; men do not ask for help; men cannot admit hurt or pain; men do not say "I can't." There is an apprehension that if a man does shed tears, or asks for help, or says that he hurts or has pain, or says "I can't," he will be viewed as weak. Being viewed as weak carries the message that he is not a real man. Real men do not cry, ask for help, express hurt, or say, "I can't." Real men suck it up. Real men "get it done."

When men experience these unrealistic expectations, it is healthier to acknowledge their humanity, rather than bow to the expectations. Humans have these thoughts and feelings. Thoughts and feelings are part and parcel of who we are.

Being able to say, "I am sad, I need help, I can't, or I am hurting," opens the door to consider how you will respond to this part of your humanity. Rather than running from, or burying such experiences, embrace them as what makes you unique. Find helpful ways to engage your thoughts and feelings. Who are those people you can trust with these feelings—friends, spouses, cleric, therapist? What are the settings in which you can express your feelings—scripture study class, support group, therapy, civic club, hobby group?

THE DEEPEST SELF AND CULTURE

Our culture and social context are critical components of our identity, and shape how we perceive the world. It is painfully clear that we have lost touch with our culture, and we see how that loss tragically unfolds in the current events around us.

The world is perceived and experienced variously by varied cultures. Not only do distinct cultures perceive the world differently, but the world is also different among cultural groups. Whatever our culture, now is the time for each of us to get in touch with our culture, and social context. Our culture reflects our first language, skin color, ethnicity, country of origin, music and diet, history, observances, and religion. Social context has to do with education, type of profession or employment, socioeconomic factors, locality, neighborhood, family, friends, neighborhood affiliations, ethnicity, political association, and nationality.

Our self-identity largely determines the world we inhabit. The world of the white person is different from the world of a person of color. The different worlds of a white person and a person of color go beyond noting and appreciating the ethnicity, and traditions of other cultures. The foods, beverages, music, and celebrations of other cultures are broadly enjoyed. Sadly, the obvious difference of color—white people and people of color—is the basis of a deep-seated prejudice.

Physical violence is the tragic and extreme expression of this prejudice. Black males, youth, and adults are subject to being shot to death. These shootings all too often are at the hands of white law enforcement officers. Black males inhabit a world where they must be vigilant, constantly on guard to protect their personal safety, and their very lives. The judicial system is another threat, as black males and males of color have a disproportionate representation in the prison population.

Law enforcement is learning both how out of touch white officers are with their ethnicity, and its influence and impact on their behavior as officers of the law. White officers urgently need to get in touch with their culture's biases to alter what they think, and how they feel about people of color.

Violence against people of color is a continuum, seen in physical violence as well as in name-calling, racial slurs, and racial epitaphs. Violence occurs in paying lower salaries to people of color, or stereotyping them as only capable of fulfilling certain roles, and holding certain occupations. This violence shows up in inadequate funding for school buildings and social service programs in areas predominately inhabited by people of color.

It matters that each of us get in touch with our culture. What limits or possibilities do my cultural facts place upon me? What privileges are mine without asking, simply because of my ethnicity? Where do I find obstacles and barriers because I am a member of a certain ethnic group? Do people assume that I speak a certain language because of my color? Do they wonder if I am a US citizen, or an undocumented person, because of my color? Do people hold some grudge against me because my last name is one from another nation? What sense of pride is mine because of the legacy of my culture? What guilt or remorse do I carry given the past acts of oppression and aggression of my culture against other cultures? What mutuality and commonality with other humans come to the forefront of my questioning?

It serves us well to get in touch with these disparate features of who we are—embodied, mammal, gender, culture. Examining the spectrum of who we are by focusing on one, and then the other component, deepens our self-understanding. Our family and personal history, our culture and social context, our shape and size, our education and experience, our nation and region, our religion and life-view, merit deliberate analysis.

The more closely we sort and examine these hues, the more profound our realization and marvel are that our self is greater than the sum of these hues. Consider how the distinct colors we see in the sky following rain, collectively create a rainbow. When you get in touch with that which you term "myself," what are the colors of your rainbow?

PURPOSE AND TOUCH

DIRECTION AND TOUCH

Purpose is the direction for our lives, knowing that we are going somewhere in contrast to milling about, going nowhere. When we awaken to, and are in touch with, the purpose of life in general, and to our personal life's own individual purpose, we know that we are on the right track. We are going somewhere. We have a direction in life, and are filled with vitality by being in touch with it.

Purpose fuels our plans. By being in touch with our purpose, we think and plan, plotting our steps along life's path to draw closer to our destination. Absent purpose, we are aimless, walking in circles, forming irregular patterns in the sands of life. When we lose touch with purpose, we not only meander, but are energy depleted. Being out of touch with purpose renders us prone to a state of malaise.

Sometimes we find that we have not lost touch with our purpose. Rather, we discover that our purpose is being transformed by degrees, not abrupt breaks. For example, when our children begin school, they come under the influence of a bigger world than the one of our home and family. We wonder about our purpose as the parents of school age children, who no longer need us in the way they did as preschoolers. With their needs being different, our purpose requires reexamination, and modifying.

Purpose as parents is transformed when our children are "grown and flown," presenting parents with the question "What is our parenting purpose with an adult child?" At this point in life, the relationship is that of adult to adult, and parenting takes on more the purpose of being a mentor, or wise and beloved friend to our adult child.

Our sense of purpose may be poignantly diminished by the death of a loved one: sibling, parent, or spouse. The death of one of our family members is a heart-rending disappearance of purpose requiring profound, and often sad revisions of lost purposes. New purposes present themselves uninvited following the death of a spouse, such as now living as a single person rather than a couple, a seismic shift after fifty years of marriage.

Once, we knew the purpose involved in relating to our sibling, our parent, or our spouse. Absent the physical presence of that loved one, we are cut free from our mooring lines, and are adrift. The signal of our diminished purpose are the questions "What am I to do? How am I going to manage? What will become of me without her/him?" or more starkly, "How can I go on living without her/him—what is the point?"

It is one thing to be meeting with an academic advisor, or a career counselor, or meditating while meeting with a spiritual director, and asking about your purpose in life. It is markedly another thing to wrestle with this question while battling storms in your work setting; or, reaching a birthday mile marker that starkly reminds you that life is rushing along; or, finding yourself without ocean trade winds to billow your sails, leaving you dead in the water—desperate and deflated.

Here is a personal example that illustrates the dynamics of an unexpected loss of purpose. I was the director of chaplaincy services for the state's largest integrated health care system from 1994 to 2012, a span of eighteen years. My plan was to work in this role until I retired. In 2012, I was sixty-seven. This retirement plan rather abruptly began to be beyond my reach, as both the chaplain staff and my supervisor began to call my "leadership" into question. I was blindsided by this alignment and coalition of staff and supervisor. All my previous supervisors had given me "outstanding" on my annual performance evaluations, as did my current supervisor in my most recent annual review.

There were months of turmoil and drama as I attempted to work with my supervisor to correct the situation, thinking initially that my supervisor was an ally in my efforts. I discovered to my sorrow and dismay that my assessment was ill-founded. Eventually, it was clear that I was about to be assigned to an untenable work situation, so I resigned, and took my retirement. I was depressed by this turn of events, and by the behavior of those who I thought respected me, and could be trusted. Here I was, sixty-seven, and wanting to continue contributing to patients, families, and staff, finding myself suddenly retired.

Eventually, I was offered a job with a local hospice as a grief counselor, or "Bereavement Coordinator." This role gave me an outlet to use my gifts and abilities as a pastoral counselor. It took some time for the pain to subside, and for the wounds of this experience to scar over, and heal.

Our own loss of health, resulting in a reduction of mental and/or physical abilities, or a change in our physical appearance, has an impact on our purpose. "I only have one arm. I have a prosthetic leg. They removed my prostate, and I have erectile dysfunction. They removed my ovaries, and I lost the ability to bear children." Given the "altered-me," what is my purpose today?

Purpose is by no means limited to humans. It is a dynamic that we share with life. Life itself has purpose. Consider for a moment this thought; what is alive has a drive to stay alive, to be living. Nature itself is alive. That is its purpose: to be. This planet, our solar system, our galaxy, and the cosmos itself exist, thrive, and flourish. Life has an astonishing drive to perpetuate itself. Life is the irreplaceable, bare essential and basic direction of reality. Life intends to be.

There is a debate among scientists regarding two colliding hypotheses about the universe. One side of the debate argues, and presents data, to support their theory that the universe is contracting. This process is a collapsing inward phenomenon. The other theory contends that the universe is expanding. In this theory, the universe continues to evolve and enlarge. Of course, in six billion years our sun will explode, destroying our solar system, and our planet, a given in science that in some ways makes the debate over how the universe will end somewhat academic for our solar system.

There is consensus that our universe presently is continuing to expand. That is to say, the universe itself manifests a purpose to thrive and flourish. It is extending itself, doing so until at some end point, the laws of physics and thermodynamics dominate, and the universe ultimately collapses. Finitude, as seen in limits and boundaries, is a feature of all creation. Within those bounds, life pulses and pushes onward.

When a human, or an ecosystem or a star, loses its drive to thrive, or loses its spirit, death results. The failure to thrive in a human culminates in death. The failure to thrive in an ecosystem culminates in stagnant ponds, dead forests, dry rivers, deserts, and dead seas. A star that fails to thrive morphs into a black hole. Perhaps, as with all living things, death, universally understood, is an inevitability.

On the level of our everyday life, we too, have a drive to thrive. Purpose is wired into us. We come that way from our mother's womb—purpose built in, part of our genetic code. One of the first actions of a newborn infant is to take a breath! Crying helps the newborn baby take rapid and deep breaths. "Stay alive," "Get those cells to dividing," "Let's move that O2," "Pump that blood ASAP," "Marshall those white blood cells STAT"—these are our physiological, hormonal, electrical, synaptic marching orders!

Our bodies are committed to keeping us alive, and work hard, at times at a herculean level, to stay alive. We want to be alive, for in being alive, all else depends—sight, hearing, sustenance, human companionship, reproduction, joy, sorrow, gratitude, failure, and fulfillment.

What does purpose have to do with touch? Being in touch with our purpose is energizing. Purpose helps us to be excited about what we are doing, and where we are going in life. When we are in touch with our purpose, we have focus. That focus is locked onto our destination, and we keep an eye on our path to ensure it leads us in the right direction.

Our life's purpose calls out, "Hey, . . . head this way—take this path." So, it is that we discover our purpose. Purpose is not crafted: it is proffered. Purpose is a gift, a treasure discovered. Purpose is akin to the North Pole, which transmits a magnetic power. That magnetic energy pulls all compasses to it. There is no question about where lies north. North is not constructed, or manufactured by human hands. No, north predates us, and owes no debt to humans.

While the North Pole tells us what direction is north, it does not provide a map of the terrain that leads through deserts and forests, and over plains and mountains. Nor does the North Pole provide a supplies and provisions list. It is up to us to determine our actual direction in relation to the North Pole (east, west, south?), and the specific supplies and provisions required for our journey. Purpose pulls at us, leaving us to craft the specifics and details.

Purpose fires the synapses in our brain, lighting up the screens of our imaginations with alluring visions. The music of purpose visits our ears, and the melody so intrigues us that we want to find its source. Our hearts are stirred and warmed, as a passion kicks off its covers, puts its feet on the floor, and begins to send excitement and energy coursing through us. Purpose calls our name. The next move is ours.

For some people, their initial purpose sets their life's course until death. They are single-minded and focused on their purpose, never deviating from that path. Others find that their initial sense of purpose undergoes a metamorphosis. The direction they take comes upon an interesting intersection, a traffic jam, an unsurpassable mountain, or a washed away bridge. Such instances may range from the intriguing, to the catastrophic.

The intrigue is that a new direction appears in our life, and we take that route to a new destination. This new direction is an epiphany. Some new purpose is revealed to us. This new purpose generates energy and excitement. Such an epiphany, or revelation, certainly occurs more than once in our lifetime.

The catastrophic loss of purpose is unwelcome and unexpected. We find ourselves at an impasse, perhaps immobilized, and certainly thrown off balance, if not knocked down. Given the degree of disequilibrium such disruptions generate, we do our best to rethink our current purpose. Such deliberation may lead to taking a detour, or rerouting. Or we may discover that what we need is a new purpose. These unexpected pauses and disruptions may open our eyes, ears, hearts, and minds to the invitation a new purpose offers.

Sometimes our purpose slowly drifts farther and farther away, until one day, we awaken and realize we have lost touch with our purpose. The loss seems sudden, although in truth, it was a slow, creeping, out-of-sight process. Most of us have moments when we drift from our purpose. It is not helpful to heap sharp criticism on yourself, or hurl words of heated blame at yourself. It is more beneficial to acknowledge the distance now between you and your purpose. With that acknowledgment, you can ask, "How will I get back in touch with what gives my life purpose?"

The answer may be, "Be still!" When life's lulls come, or a catastrophe strikes, frantic activity will create motion, and not one iota of movement. The appropriate response is to be quiet, to listen, to be receptive, to be attentive. Life's winds will stir again. Purpose will appear, and exert its pull on us, moving us with every increasing momentum in its direction.

These disruptions, whether an opportunity, a catastrophe, or a mere drifting away, are no simple challenge, and typically involve some pain. There is grief over a purpose lost, and the grief is to be respected and honored. The grief is not a signal of weakness ("get over it"). Grief is a sign that your purpose was valued, and mattered deeply to you.

Sometimes the loss of purpose creates a sense of failure. It is no surprise that we may feel like we failed when we do not reach our destination, or attain our original purpose. Calling oneself a "failure" when powers beyond our making and control collapse the overpass required to reach our destination, is a harsh, and unrealistic criticism. If our own behavior is the cause for us no longer having access to the subway to our life's destination, it is more helpful to accept responsibility than to berate and disparage ourselves.

In any case, when we do realize that the path we are taking is no longer appealing or available, failure is not the conclusion. Rather, when our life's purpose disappears, and what we envision is as unavailable to us as is driving our car to Mars, that situation is a moment of learning. We learn that the purpose to which we felt called no longer appeals, or is unattainable. There is nothing bad or lacking about us. We simply learn that the goal we had in mind for our lives needs replacing. We learn that we do not possess the aptitude, the discipline, the interests, the cognitive skills, the passion, or the personality required of people in that field.

Again, such learning is not evaluative: it is descriptive. Not all of us are going to play professional athletics. Not all of us are going to win the Noble Prize in science or the arts. Not all of us are going to win the Pulitzer Prize for our literary accomplishments. Not everybody has what it takes to be a cook, let alone a chef. And so on.

Each of these realizations on our part is an honest self-survey that provides a truer analysis of our strengths and our deficits. Our society's notion that we "can be whatever we want to be" is both a truth and a cruel falsehood. Yes, in this nation, we are free to pursue our life's goals and fulfill our ambitions. No caste system, be it socioeconomic, ethnic, gender, cultural (yes, the current cruel prejudices are a stark reality, be they unlawful and immoral), are able in this country to lock and bar doors legally. That is relatively true, as we know that money, color, culture, gender, height, appearance are realities as we pursue our dreams.

The falsehood is that we do not all possess the requisite gifts to steer our lives toward some purposes. Some people have the intellect, the aptitude, the physical attributes and coordination, the "eye" or the "ear" that others do not. Some painters have what it takes to do commercial or residential painting, and some painters possess what it takes to do oil and canvas, or watercolors.

It is foolish to compare our purpose with that of someone else. There is no ranking of purposes. People of courage, morals, and fortitude are spread across the landscape of life. Your purpose serves in a grand manner, for you are contributing and making a difference in life. There is no one in the universe like you. No one brings the energy, the ideas, the smile, and the abilities to life that reside in you. Life would be the lesser without you. Every day, in every interaction, you are shaping and molding others, making an impact on the cosmos. You may not know in your lifetime the outcome accomplished in life that is connected directly to you.

It is the case that we can do many things with our lives. Those options rest on an honest appraisal and assessment of our interests and abilities. You are blessed by having an array of paths. Viewing these many paths, yours is the task to weigh and select the most appealing and alluring one—the one that exerts a strong pull, and draws you to it.

That strong pull may lead to an insight. There are those who became an attorney, and were drawn in that direction, only to discover that law was not their earnest interest. Some find speed skating extraordinarily appealing, and quickly learn that they lack the fundamental and requisite mental and physical abilities—and really do not like the cold temperatures that are part and parcel of an ice rink.

These discoveries are a gift, not a goof. The sooner we learn that what looked like such a promising course for our life is unappealing, the better. There is no need, no valor, and no wisdom in staying with a course that inflicts pain and misery upon us.

I wanted to be a popular trumpet player—an age-appropriate fantasy for a teenager. Well—I am no Maynard Ferguson, Winton Marsalis, Dizzy Gillespie, Miles Davis, or Maurice Andre. Fortunately, I realized that truth during my senior year of high school. My life could have been sad absent this honest self-appraisal and acknowledgment. My attitude is one of gratitude that I was honest about my self-discipline and abilities, and with that realization, allowed life's breezes to fill my sails with winds blowing in another direction. Instead of fighting that breeze, I allowed it to fill my life's sails, and propel me toward a new destination.

Is your purpose to be a musician, an artist, a builder of buildings, an educator, an athlete, an electrician, a wordsmith, a chef, a religious leader, or to serve our nation in uniform or elected office? Other purposes await us—to be a loving spouse, a caring parent, a supportive friend, a solid employee, a trusted professional.

Purpose is bigger than work, jobs, and careers. Some of life's foundational purposes are spiritual growth and development, moral and ethical fitness, integrity, strength of character, developing empathy, and cultivating compassion. These purposes are those that are the cornerstone of our professional and personal lives and pursuits. Blessed is the person who is in touch with the summoning call of purpose.

RETIREMENT AND TOUCH

Retirement is an occasion where individuals lose touch with their purpose. A good many individuals, men and women, find their purpose in their work. Who they are, is what they do! Employees say, "I am an engineer; I am a truck driver; I am a backhoe operator; I am a financial advisor." These statements reveal the conflation of work and identity: we are our job. These comments merge work and purpose. Our job is our purpose. Our purpose is our job.

Sadly, what was generally true for men is increasingly prominent among women professionals and employees. It appears that the loss of purpose among retirees is contagious, spreading quickly among men and women alike. When retirement comes to such men—and women—and come it will, they are at sea, completely out of touch with the coastline of purpose.

My wife and I both retired in June of 2018. At that time, I had a job as a family therapist in a private mental health clinic. I was experiencing growing stress in that setting. In discussing and describing my stress to my psychiatrist, and its resultant impact on me, my psychiatrist said in no uncertain terms that I needed to resign immediately, that very day!

I was doing my best to manage my stress, and now faced the reality that my efforts were not sufficient to maintain my well-being. I actually wanted to work a bit more, and had some reservations about resigning. These reservations were outvoted by the toll the stress was taking on me, and by my psychiatrist's concern for my health.

I went to the clinic, and talked to the administrator. I explained my situation, concluding my remarks with the statement that "my doctor has ordered me to resign, effective today." The administrator expressed hopes that I could stay on, going on to accept gracefully my resignation.

In the days that followed, my depression heightened. I saw myself as being without a purpose. As a 1099 contractor, I was able to do some piece work as that became available, which was somewhat helpful. I was just above the bottom of the barrel. I found that retirement is not a cake walk, and was unprepared for the shock and loss of purpose (personal, spiritual, professional).

Today finds me in a better spot, as I realize that I am multi-purposed. My purposes are husband, father, grandfather, relative, friend, author, trumpet player, spiritual way-finder. My 1099 contract work continues, and brings me satisfaction. Every so often I miss the purpose that comes with employment, but that quickly passes!

Purpose gives our lives direction. A compass tells us the direction of our travel, but does not provide a detailed map. A sextant tells us where we are on our journey, failing to tell us how to reach our destination. The stars are ancient friends, placing before us our destination, yet not giving any hint of the detailed characteristics of the land or water paths that will usher us to our destination. No matter—it is essential that we stay in touch with our direction. We can handle the step-by-step efforts of the journey!

Purpose gives us a goal. Traveling to that goal means moving out into the depths of life, establishing roots, creating relationships, acquiring requisite education and training, disciplining our management of time and effort, enduring the inevitable storms or stills, building resilience and grit, and staying on course. Being true to our purpose means facing tragedies and hardships so that our spirituality is deepened. It means facing temptation, being anchored by our morals and ethics. We expand our compassion so that the pursuit of our purpose includes seeing the needs of others, offering help and support.

MEANING AND TOUCH

M eaning is how we make sense of the world. Being in touch
with our sense of meaning helps us approach the splintered
and shattered shards of life, and keep a coherent and cohered
world. It is how we suffer life's tragedies, and keep going. It is our
shock absorber, taking the full impact of life's jarring blows, yet
enabling us to rebound. Meaning permits us to answer life's big
questions: Why am I here? How do I view death? What does love
offer, and require of me?

Each person has a unique way to construct meaning, and
thereby be able to think and feel that life is meaning-full. This
framework enables us to cope with life's triumphs and tragedies,
events that attack our sense that life is meaning-full. For instance,
when our long-standing friend is killed in a freak freeway vehicu-
lar accident, what meaning do we ascribed to his death? Is the
crash simply a wreck at freeway speeds, an everyday event in any
city, or an injustice to universal ethical principles? If you or a family member has a heart attack, what meaning do you bring to that
loss of health? Is a heart attack merely a medical event, one that is
common in our society; or is it a matter of life being unfair?

In truth, we each see the world uniquely, and "make sense"
of the world in the manner that best suits us. We make sense of
the world with the building materials we as a nation, society, and
culture hold in common. For example, the Constitution and the

Declaration of Independence are shared cornerstones for making sense in the United States of America.

Likewise, a good many people hold in common religious resources of meaning. In these instances, the shared trust in a Greatest Mystery (God, Creator, Sacred Spirit, Transcendent Other), an essential sacred scripture (Bible, Koran, Tanakh), key formative sacred stories (Creation, Exodus, Exile, Homecoming, Messiah, Crucifixion, and Resurrection), and foundation teachings (Ten Commandments, Great Commandment, Golden Rule, Two Great Commandments, Sermon on the Mount) are held in common among members of the faith community. These primary meaning resources establish bonds within the community, and are invaluable to making sense. They put us in touch with a steadying and guiding meaning.

Combined with these held-in-common resources for meaning, are the individual's unique resources. Individuals draw upon their culture, gender, socioeconomic status, and family to shape how they in their distinct manner find meaning in life. While we certainly depend on held-in-common perspectives to find meaning, beyond that we require our personal and distinct way of finding life to be meaning-full.

We are aware that being in touch with our sense of meaning is essential to making sense of life's stark realities. I witnessed terminally ill, dying patients, making varied comments about their pending deaths to their health care team, to their friends, and families. There are those patients, who in the face of their imminent death, are peaceful, content, and at rest. They say things like: "I am OK; I will be fine; Don't worry about me; Life has been good to me; I am so blessed."

Other patients remark: "I am being cheated out of the best years of my life; I will never get to take that trip; Those doctors should have done something earlier to help me; Life has never been fair to me; I was dealt a bad hand!"

The way we assemble the world makes sense to us, and generally serves us well. Our framing of the world meets most of life's unexpected and unexplainable events. Then there comes a tsunami, a horrendous wave of fearsome power. It plays with mighty ships as though they were toys, and dashes ashore to wreak havoc on buildings of all sorts, ripping holes in earth's fabric as well. No ship, no sea wall, no human-constructed edifice can withstand the tsunami's mighty wrecking ball.

Tsunamis smash into our everyday lives. These tsunamis flatten us personally, devastate strangers, or rain mayhem on our loved ones. Senseless murderous mass shootings at night clubs, schools, concerts, movie theaters, churches, mosques, synagogues, and resort hotels, killing innocent and unsuspecting children and adults, are a force of horror, sweeping us away.

Our family member developing ALS, Alzheimer's, or Parkinson's Disease, pulls the rug out from under us, putting us flat on the ground. We lose touch with our meaning in such instances, as our hands are not powerful enough to hold onto our sense of meaning in the tug-of-war with these tragedies. How *do* we make sense of such horror? *Can* we make sense of such mayhem?

Most of us repair or replace our structure of meaning by finding usable building blocks among the rubble. Stone by stone, we go about the arduous task of building a new way of making sense of the world, a new way of seeing meaning in life. Depression is one sign of someone being unable to reconstruct a framework of meaning. A world without meaning is a shadowy world indeed.

Life sometimes is meaningless! There are those moments which defy human power to find even a single grain of meaning. How do we make sense of the assassination of beloved political leaders? How do we find meaning in a frightful disease that takes the life of an influential scientist? When individually or collectively we are pounded by mind-boggling senselessness, what do we do? A friend of mine would suggest that we "give consent."

When we consent to what makes no sense, we are neither lashing out in anger, nor crumpling in surrender—two common human responses to the senseless. Consent is the courageous recognition that life does not always add up. Consent studies the jagged tear in a favorite garment, concluding that no tailor will be able to mend and repair that rip. Consent stands over a shattered,

77

treasured vase, recognizing that it is impossible to put it back together. Consent sits next to the hospital bed of a dear friend, her life stricken with, and being shortened by, pancreatic cancer, absorbing the fact that there is no cure for this cancer. It will inevitably end your friend's life.

Consent is the alternative to despair and angry cynicism, given the senselessness rampant in life. Planes crash, killing entire athletic teams and their coaches. Rivers leap out of their confining banks, tearing through main street, sweeping to death a would-be rescuer. Fires rage, in the United States and abroad, turning to ash forests, homes, businesses, killing bold firefighters, and vulnerable wildlife. A child riding with her parents is struck in the head by a bullet intended for her father. Law enforcement officers sitting in their patrol unit are ambushed and killed. A black man reaching into his jacket to produce his wallet as commanded, is shot to death doing exactly what the officer ordered him to do. School children sitting in class are gunned down, as are their teachers and administrators.

Such events do stir anger. How could such a thing happen? These sorrows do bring the dark clouds of grief. If we are not angry, and if we are not sad, then we do not get it. This anger and sorrow, understandably arising in the aftermath of senseless human acts, or the blind power of nature, subside over time—generally. Lacking a framework to make consent possible, our option is to become an angry person. Not a person who is experiencing anger, but an angry, cynical individual. Or being unable to consent to the sheer granite face that is tragedy, we become a morose person. No longer are we experiencing sadness; rather, we are a sullen, sulking, sad individual. Both cynicism and sullenness are unhealthy, threatening our physical, mental, emotional, and spiritual wellbeing. We may find ourselves an angry grump, or a sad grump. In either case, we become a grump.

When life appears to contradict meaning, consent is the healing path. Consent embraces the anger, and sits down with sorrow. Consent is realistic. We cannot consent to a fairy-tale world. Consent is not wishful thinking, unrealistic, or fact-fleeing. Consent feels the full impact of tragedy, staggering and stunned by its blows. It considers bravely, truthfully, and honestly the depths of the senseless horror.

This honest appraisal makes it possible to say, "Yes, this situation is sickeningly senseless, full of sorrow. Even so, life is good. Life is worth living. We will get through this. Such abhorrent events happen, and will happen again." These tragedies are not the norm, but an aberration. There is no explanation, and no way to make sense of what happened. The important question for moving through this tragedy is not "Why did this happen," as if there were an explanation that would help.

The real question is, "What are we going to do since it did happen?" The "what" question is the bedrock for processing the tragedy in a health-achieving manner. Regarding school shootings, the "What are we going to do?" question finds those who favor "hardening" the school's protective physical features: barriers at the front entrance, secure and bullet-proof doors at the entrance, security cameras throughout the building, sturdier classroom doors with heavy-duty locks.

There are further proposals. Some propose arming the teachers, with only those teachers who undergo specific training allowed to carry weapons in the schools. Others insist that improved mental health services need to be available and accessible.

There are those in the population of the mind that something must done about rapid-fire, multiple-round rifles that are combat rifle knockoffs of battlefield mass casualty weapons. Movie theaters, night clubs, churches, synagogues, casinos, and shopping centers have seen what these weapons can do. Proposals for what must be done include a tighter process for proving eligibility for a gun license; banning the production of such weapons; requiring that these particular weapons be modified by the manufacturer to be less a military weapon, and more a sporting firearm; holding the manufacturer legally and financially responsible for mass shootings.

Various schools and school districts are implementing changes to improve student security. Private properties are doing what they can do to add armed guards, and tighten security measures. One church in Texas recently was in the news when the church's security staff shot and killed an armed, menacing, and threatening worshipper. Unfortunately, our nation remains at an impasse over what to do across the country about automatic, rapid-fire, multiple-round weapons. What, as a nation, can we expect with our inaction?

For our nation to process in a healthy manner past mass shootings requires that we face these tragedies head-on. There are several options by which the number of incidents, and the number of casualties can be reduced. These steps provide the basis for a new meaning, one that says, "We refuse to stand idly by in the face of mass shootings. We are taking appropriate, and preventive steps to minimize the occurrence and impact of this social ill. A mass shooting may be attempted in the future. If so, we will learn from it, and improve the precautions we have in place. We consent to the presence of evil, and commit ourselves to confronting and thwarting it."

Some people find that their power to confront this evil stems from their outlook that "things will work out." There are people with the capacity to say, "It will be okay," or, "We will get through this somehow." Such phrases come from deep within those persons. These comments, or mottoes, are far from being flip or casual. You can feel the tangible seriousness in their voice. You sense the courage required to confront reality so honestly.

Ironically, the way we make and find meaning in our life in the face of injustice, must be able to contend with meaninglessness, with chaos, with the inexplicable. We need the capacity to hold together the both/and of life. Life is both meaningful and meaningless at times. Life is not an either/or proposition. An either/or approach contends that life is meaningful, or it is not. There are no two ways about it.

This either/or approach is rigid, and brittle. Either/or cannot manage life's contradictions or tragedies. This persuasion sees the world as black and white. It is a dualistic mindset of oil and water, good and evil, right, and wrong. Such thinking has no patience with complexity, multi-dimensions, or the "gray" in life where black and white lap at each other's shores.

People of this persuasion find themselves having to locate some "higher purpose" in the injustices in life. What higher purpose is there in the injustice of the millions of people forced to leave their homeland in search of another nation where they are safe from warfare and famine; or the injustice of civilians killed by a chemical weapon unleashed on them by their own government; or the random terror of forest fires devouring forests, homes, animal and human life like a roaring dragon of flame? Attempts to find a "higher purpose" in such horror comes across as disconnected with reality, and dismissive of human misery, and the planet's pain. The "either/or" approach is doomed to cynicism or irrationality. It is an approach built on sand.

A house of meaning built on sand is unable to withstand the assaults of chaos. Life will bring torrents of the unexplainable, the contradictory, and the absurd. What is required for us to construct a house of meaning that can withstand these inevitable torrents? Our structure of meaning requires an "in-spite-of" quotient in establishing meaning in life at large, and in our personal lives. The in-spite-of perspective provides a foundation of rock for meaning's house.

Thankfully, tsunamis are rare events. We find life meaning-full most of the time. Looking at our marriage, we conclude that it is a rewarding relationship, providing mutual enrichment. It is a relationship offering us and our partner companionship and acceptance. We look at our work, and do not see drudgery. Our work appears to us as a genuine venue where we sense that our efforts count, that we are making a difference, and that we are contributing. We survey all the brokenness and injustice scattered about the world, and discern a meaningful world in-spite-of the disarray and destruction. These are the reassuring moments when we know that we are in touch with our structures of meaning.

RELATIONSHIPS AND TOUCH

INTERDEPENDENCE AND TOUCH

Life is relational. Creation itself is a constellation of relationships, grand and minute. Nothing stands abstracted. Nothing exists alone, in isolation, out of touch with everything else. Humans breathe in the O_2 produced by plants, and plants absorb the CO_2 generated by humans. This relationship is symbiotic in that humans and plants each need and require what the other produces. Ants and aphids likewise have a reciprocal and symbiotic relationship. The aphids produce a food substance for the ants, and the ants protect the aphids from predators such as ladybugs and lacewings.

Another image for the relationships in life is that of the spider web. The spider creates the web to serve its own ends. The strands on the web demonstrate relationships. A spider web is constructed on the basis of relationships, as one strand is connected to every other strand. What happens on one strand of the spider's web is felt along each and every strand, such that the whole web vibrates. The spider and its web give us a lesson from nature regarding our interdependence. What affects one, affects all.

At the level of our green garden, Earth, everything is related to, and connected to, everything else. The oceans, rivers, atmosphere, wind, soil, greenery, animals, humans, insects, reptiles, mammals, fish, whales, mountains, deserts are inseparable. All things affect all things. We simply must stay in touch with this interdependence. Many of these relationships are symbiotic.

Chief Seattle's attributed words are timely, succinct, and true:

> This we know: All things are connected
> like the blood which unites one family.
> All things are connected.
> Whatever befalls the earth befalls the sons of the earth.
> Man did not weave the web of life.
> He is merely a strand on it.
> Whatever he does to the web, he does to himself.
> (Attributed to Chief Seattle, 1854)

Our human body is a microcosm of the macrocosm that is our world of relationships. Our bodies are constituted of individual cells which relate to other cells, forming organs and systems, all intertwined and related to sustain bodily life. The Apostle Paul uses the metaphor of the human body to make a point about living in a particular arrangement of relationships, e.g., a congregation. He writes:

> If the whole body were an eye, where would the hearing be? If the whole body were hearing, where would the sense of smell be? If all were a single member, where would the body be? As it is there are many members, yet one body. (1 Cor 2:17–20 NRSV)

There are those who like to be in touch with their relationships in a unique manner. These persons we call introverts. They seek solitude more than human companionship. These individuals may be known to us in our circles of acquaintance, those who prefer to stay to themselves, and generally are content with their own company. In their solitude, they do interact, and experience a semblance of societal touch with a variety of others. That touch is experienced in a multitude of settings: work, school, stores, the internet or social media, public transit, repair persons, or house of worship.

Extroverts are people who prefer to be in touch with their relationships. They enjoy social interaction, and enjoy being with people more than they enjoy being alone. Yet, on occasion, extroverts sense that they are out of touch in their relationships, relationships ranging from their intimate others, family, to friends, and neighbors. While these experiences of being out of touch particularly with our intimate others and family are intermittent, they are painful when they appear. Try as we may in these moments of lost touch, we find it difficult if not impossible to reestablish touch in these moments with our important others.

Encountering difficulty as we put energy and effort into our attempts to restore touch, we may finally be able to identify what it is that makes restoring touch difficult in our relationships. The obstacle to touch may be a profound clash, which remains unresolved, and the residue of this clash hangs in the air like an unpleasant odor. It may be a difference of generations, differences which have their unique markers and traits. We may attribute the obstacle to different socioeconomic levels, which work against finding a common ground for conversation and coffee.

Today, we find ourselves in a sea change of society, politics, technology, culture, health care, spirituality, and realize how out of touch with our relationships we are at multiple levels. There is roughly one-third of the nation who have lost touch with the previous world they knew. They liked that world, and nostalgically long for its return. This "used-to-be world" is one prior to environmental impacts and concerns, civil rights, empowered females, the drastic loss of the middle class, the emergence of the "1-percenters," and the increased prominence and presence of people of color. These and others enormous changes are shifting the bases and sources of power in our nation.

Others in the population feel out of touch with the present political, economic, and environmental eddies. These individuals see the world they once knew being eroded. That world was one of community, inclusion, respect for the Constitution, Congress, the judicial system, freedom of the press, and the rule of law. They see the current fear and divisions, the untruths, and falsehoods, and long to restore touch with the world of justice, peace, tolerance, with liberty and justice for all.

Closer to home, we gaze at our children, including adult children. We look at our grandchildren and great-grandchildren. What do we see? We see the prevalence of electronic devices and gadgets, different clothes, diverse ways of dressing, "strange" hair styles and colors. We listen to the way that they talk, and observe their values. What we see and hear results in our feeling so out of touch.

Work is no different. Young or old, we feel out of touch with our work team. We see people arriving late to work, or people who stay past quitting, and we wonder, "What's with that?" We are in the midst of people in a meeting who are looking down and texting one another; or, persons who see the meeting as the setting where work teams can look at each other, and talk through things, and we scratch our heads: "Really?" The informal attire of some of the work team strikes us as disrespectful, and the business attire of some strikes us as "stuffy." We notice the contemporary practice of jumping from job to job, in contrast to being a longtime, and loyal employee. In either instance, the question emerges, "What are you thinking?" Young and old find it laborious to get in touch with one another, and with the respective and different worlds. Going to work becomes quite tedious when we find ourselves out of touch in our workplace.

INTIMATES AND TOUCH

The paramount relationship is with our intimate others. These intimate relations take many forms: long-term relationships; committed relationships; marriages; partnerships; and significant others. These relationships all are created by the couple, who are devoted and dedicated to the well-being of the other, and the relationship itself. Do you sense that you have lost touch with what holds and bonds your intimate relationships? Do you sense that you and your partner are out of touch?

Is it possible that you have lost touch with an ancient and universal teaching: "Love your neighbor as you love yourself" (Lev 19:18c NRSV)? This commandment reaches beyond the relationship with the intimate other to include everyone. While it reaches beyond the intimate other, it certainly speaks to that relationship. The commandment directs us to love others by recognizing their humanity and divine image.

Touch is the common denominator among intimates. The intimates are in touch with their commitments, and their thoughts and feelings for the other. Husbands and wives, and partners touch one another's hearts, souls, minds, and bodies. They are open and transparent, baring their innermost self to the other, a trusting and tender intimacy, reserved and preserved for the intimate other. They are in touch with a common history, and in touch with the contours of the relationship in its current form. Further, they are in touch with shared hopes for a promising and rewarding future. Your intimate relationships are dynamic, evolving and blossoming with new patterns and colors, as long as you stay in touch with the wisdom of "love your neighbor as yourself."

Intimate couples first and foremost deeply respect and revere the "thou" of their beloved. They know that their beloved is a distinct and unique person, and they prize that uniqueness. Intimates learn each other's life stories and history, and enjoy the personality that distinguishes their beloved. They respect the perspective and interests of their beloved, and let those stand without efforts to change them. Couples admire the values and goals of the beloved, and do their best to honor those values, and support the pursuit of those goals.

Intimates express their devotion to the beloved by extending and receiving grace and forgiveness. Intimates say to themselves, "I am not perfect." They say to one another, "You are not perfect, and I love you, warts and all!" Intimates disagree, disappoint, and discourage one another.

In such moments, forgiveness restores harmony. These rough patches, and finding a way through them, are part of the history and resiliency of the relationship. These conversations exhibit loving one another as they wish to be loved. You want to be accepted "warts and all," and you want as well to accept your intimate "warts and all." Such acceptance is grace, the shield against expectations for perfection, and the immunization against pride. So, it is that intimates fashion strong bonds, and create a deep trust between them.

Intimates establish their patterns and routines for physical intimacy, those that suit and satisfy them. Life circumstances occur which put you and your partner out of touch with your accustomed expressions of intimacy. Illness, overall health, stress, and age affect and alter your physical capacities for intimacy. It is painful to be out of touch with the former powers of intimacy that now, given circumstances, are beyond your reach. New forms and patterns can be devised.

Marital relationships and the relationships of partners are intimate in kaleidoscopic ways in addition to physical expressions of intimacy. Intimates need to be in touch with the full array of intimacy, which includes the sharing of thoughts, ideas, dreams, hurts, regrets, joys, and laughter. A communication that touches your partner is one of disclosing what you think, how you reached certain conclusions, what assumptions matter to you, which of your thoughts are not fully developed and organized, and what questions for you yet remain unaddressed, or unanswered. In communicating with your intimate, you let her or him touch your heart and mind.

Intimates touch their partner's heart and soul by sharing deeply held, and deeply felt emotions. These emotions are joy, excitement, anticipation, sorrow, anger, contentment, frustration, acceptance, and worry. Touching the other with these emotions creates an authentic relationship, where the partners' actual and entire being is accessed, and shared.

It takes trust and courage for you and your loved one to talk about your feelings. Doing so requires first that you are in touch with your own feelings. Also required is the courage for you or your partner to be open and transparent so that your partner can touch extremely sensitive and tender areas of your life.

Making it hard to get in touch with your feelings is the fact that culture considers some feelings taboo. Various feelings are characterized as unbecoming, and a few feelings are catalogued as sinful. Such prohibitions are impotent to stop the presence or appearance of a feeling. Feelings are a given, and they have a life of their own, sometimes shocking or scaring us when they pop up. "Where did that come from?" is a common exclamation when feelings appear uninvited. In these moments of surprise, we feel so out of touch with ourselves.

Trust is what allows intimates to bring their private and deep feelings to their partner. You trust your partner to receive and hold your feelings with respect and empathy. If you lose touch with your trust of your partner, of if your partner loses touch with their trust of you, these deep exchanges are unlikely to happen. If you and your partner seem stuck in small talk, or silence, it may be that you have lost touch with your trust of the other.

Some feelings connect with past events of success or joy, while others are connected to fear, trauma, or pain. You and your intimate will be enriched to the degree you are in touch with these past events. Being in touch with your joys and sorrows makes you a more complete person, and allows the relating of these experiences. Narrating these events puts your intimate more in touch with the full you, and broadens and deepens your intimacy with one another.

We all have feelings that we may never disclose to our loved one, and elect to keep to ourselves. Such privacy is to be honored, and not viewed as "holding back" from the intimate other. You are in touch with these feelings, and consider that these deep and powerful feelings are best addressed in counseling or therapy. Each person determines what seems best for her or him at the time regarding these epochal feelings.

You need to be in touch with your care, courage, and commitment to present an openness to welcome and receive the emotions of your intimate. Different people find different emotions of their beloved challenging. Some stumble or falter with processing their mate's sorrow, or worry. Others have an awkward time absorbing their intimate other's anger, or discouragement. Some find it embarrassing to hear the affirmations their partner showers upon them. These challenging times and awkward moments can be somewhat eased by being in touch with your trust of your intimate.

Communication is not a technique of responsive listening, or unconditional positive regard, or conflict resolution. These abilities are important. Communication is about depth and transparency, not about technique, which is saying the right thing at the right time in the right way.

Communication, to be touching, is occasionally clumsy, often awkward, and at times difficult, requiring patience, commitment, and energy. It is arduous work to articulate some things, and some things simply defy the confines of words. Often, a look, a facial expression, a squeeze of a hand, or a hug is the language that truly communicates. That is the case as words are at times simply inadequate for the moment at hand. Sometimes silence itself is the only way to receive and honor the joy or the sorrow experienced by the intimate other. Efforts to talk at these times are ill-advised, and are not mindful of the complexity and depth present. These moments are those where physical touch is the language that communicates, and in doing so, touches the heart of the loved one. Research shows that a touch of the forearm communicates gratitude, compassion, and love.[1]

A hug or a touch on the shoulder speak their own language.[2] We know a hug that speaks compassion to us. Empathy is a unique hug. Joy requires a special hug. Those needing support hear and feel that support more often and more effectively in a hug, not words.[3]

The emotions manifested in touch, be they compassion, joy, pride, encouragement, affection, support, or empathy, are distinct and discernible one from the other. Those being touched "hear" the message contained in that physical contact, and can distinguish the feeling each hug conveys to them. Touch speaks its own language, and is a welcome supplement and expansion of our communication with those who matter the most to us.

1. Keltner, *Born to Be Good.*

2 Hertenstein et al., "Touch Communicates," 532.

3. Hertenstein et al., "Touch Communicates," 532.

Sadly, there is touch in relationships that is hurtful, and not healing. Some of us are exposed to touch that is insensitive and intrusive. This touch is never invited, welcomed, or enjoyed. The person whose privacy and personal boundaries are invaded and assaulted is disgusted, humiliated, and angered by this gross insensitivity and sheer inhumanity. It may speak more to the point to call such abusers "predators."

Harmful touch communicates disregard for the person of the other individual. Harmful touch bruises hearts, minds, spirits, and bodies. This touch is always overpowering, as it brushes aside the dignity and objections of the other. The overpowering component may draw its strength from muscle mass, a weapon, position, status, family relation, profession, work relation, influence, or rank. The power of the harmed is no match for the power of the harmer. The other is treated as an object for the intruder's pleasure, subject to the will and wishes of the offender, who is dismissive of the humanity of the other.

The most common forms of harmful touch are sexual and physical abuse. Our culture presently is rife with instances of sexual abuse, as seen in the #MeToo movement, and the numerous sexual lawsuits filling the court's dockets. The sexual predators are primarily men, who use power inequities to prey upon vulnerable and defenseless children, women, and men. These men come from the ranks of the incredibly wealthy, powerful businessmen, movie and TV executives and producers, trusted religious leaders and clergy, schoolteachers, actors, politicians, physicians, and male family members.

Some of the predators are rapists of men or women. Some of the predators are pedophiles, preying on young girls or boys. A small percentage of adult females prey on teenage minor males, engaging the boys in sexual acts. These examples of sexual abuse and predatory behavior show heartless acts. Those who experience harmful touch, find because of that trauma that they cut off touch with certain thoughts and feelings.

Psychological and physical abuse has no regard for socioeconomic status, culture, or class. It is not localized to any sociological group. Generally, it is men who are psychologically and physically abusive to their children, the children of their girlfriends, and/or to their wives and intimate others. Certainly, women are known to be psychologically and physically abusive to children, and far less so to men.

I contrast healing touch with harmful touch. A healing touch begins with acknowledging the privacy and boundaries of the intimate other. A healing touch is not a seeking touch: it is a giving touch. A healing touch has no agenda to get something from the other. Healing touch strives to give something to the intimate other, perhaps love, encouragement, support, affection. A healing touch is concerned with the "thou" of the other person, of the intimate other's personhood, dignity, and honor. I do acknowledge the presence of harmful touch, while striving to emphasize the inestimable value of healing touch.

I want to take a few moments to say a something about men and touch. Men in this country and society are largely out of touch with their feelings. Men are expected to cut off touch with their interior life. They are taught not to cry, complain, or ask for help. Men are socialized to bear life's challenges and disappointments in silence. They are allowed to be angry, and to express that anger. However, under no circumstances are they to say: "I hurt; I am sad; I can't; I need help." Men are taught to suck it up, saddle up, soldier on, shake it off, or tough it out. Is it any wonder that men face unique challenges in communicating, in touching, and in being touched?

Men will find it helpful to get in touch with their other feelings beyond anger. These other feelings are pain, hurt, sorrow, helplessness, joy, excitement, wonder, care, and compassion. The question is not "Do men have the full array of human emotions and feelings?" but "How do men get in touch with and manage the feelings they share with the rest of humanity?"

For men to acknowledge their feelings is to practice wellness. Ignored or pent-up feelings are like flood waters behind a dam. All dams have a load limit, and given enough rain and runoff, a dam will burst. It is better to open the flood gates, and lessen the water's pressure, while also preserving the integrity of the dam, and protecting the communities downstream.

Men can express their feelings with words and touch, and by listening to the feelings of their intimate others. A smile comes automatically to a man's face when he looks at his intimate other. Watching his child in the crib, or playing in the backyard, fills a man's heart with warmth. Seeing his wife agonizing in a hospital bed makes him sad and scared. He learns the limits of his ability to help, and that he needs the help of the health care team to restore his wife's health.

Feelings are not something to fear. Being in touch with your feelings is something to welcome. When a man can practice wellness by getting in touch with his feelings, and acknowledge that he is happy or sad, up or down, dejected or exhilarated, he is on the home stretch. Feelings do not require an instruction manual. They pretty much are self-operating. A happy feeling brings a smile. A sad feeling turns down the corners of your mouth. Dejection furrows the brow and turns eyes downward. Exhilaration brightens eyes, broadens grins, and puts lift in your step. All men need to do is let the feeling take its own course. Relax—it knows what to do!

Men are taught to be fixers, and helpers. Listening is not viewed as helping. I encourage men to learn that listening is doing something! I am contrasting listening as an effort to solve and fix your partner's problem, with listening in a way that you are present and caring. Your partner will ask for your help if they want it. Generally, when your intimate other asks to talk with you, what they want you to do is—listen! If it helps you, you might practice asking your intimate other if they want you to problem-solve with them, or be present, be there for them, and listen.

Listening takes work, which is why listening is doing something. You must attend to inflection, facial expression, nuances, affect, and body language to listen. Listening sends a message to your intimate other that you care, which is why listening is doing something. Listening may be holding your intimate other, quietly sitting, being secure and comfortable with the silence.

Ironically, trying to fix your partner's problem, tells your partner that they are helpless, incapable, and unable to handle their own life. Do you really want to give them that message? Instead, simply listen, which says that you respect your intimate other's ability to manage the situation, and that you are there with and for them in this moment. Try it.

FRIENDS AND TOUCH

The word "friend" means everything and nothing. We have our social media "friends," we have friends at work, and we have friends who know our depths and love us unconditionally. My discussion of friends references friends who matter, and who care about you. These friends are the ones who will drop whatever they are doing, and come to our side, no matter the time of day. These are the friends with whom we need to stay in touch.

These friends esteem our well-being, and make our interests and concerns a priority in their own lives. These are the people that we can tell anything, whom we trust with our hurts, failings, and secrets. They can see us at our worst. We will let them help us when we are ill. We tell them our fears. We confess our mistakes and wrong doings that are troubling and eating at us.

These deep friends are rare, probably somewhere in the area of three or so. The number of deep friends is inconsequential, as what matters is the depth of the friendship. These friendships know no limits, and have no end. They are a divine gift in our lives, rare and priceless.

These deep friends and friendships need a nurturing touch. We can ill-afford to lose such people from our lives. They are irreplaceable. Nurturing these friendships is critical to our well-being. That nurture requires our staying in touch via coffee, lunch, phone calls, visits, email, cards, letters. Touching our friends means remembering their birthday, anniversary, and acknowledging their joys at home and work. Our friends are incredibly important to our well-being, and our happiness is of the utmost importance to them.

When I was in the burn unit following the fire at my home, I was between jobs. I found myself between health insurance policies and salaries. My former job had as a matter of course cancelled my health insurance policy, and was no longer paying me a salary. I had not begun my new job, and the church had not initiated health insurance, nor salary. These financial considerations had me distressed.

Up stepped my friend Vernon. He was a church official and administrator in my denomination. He and his wife were then, and still are today, dear friends. Vernon understood employment and financial issues. Working with both congregations, who were supportive and caring, Vernon helped craft a smooth transition regarding my salary and health insurance. I never asked for his help. He saw the situation, and knew what was to be done.

On a societal level, we Americans need to get back in touch with the reality that we are friends far more than adversaries. We need to restore our touch with friendship for one another. We hold the same things dear, and hold each other dear. We serve one another, each in our role and station in life. Librarians, law enforcement officers, sanitation workers, civil servants, schoolteachers, laborers, trades people, politicians, jurists, parents all contribute to the well-being of one another, and our nation.

Friendship goes a long way in resolving differences. Conversations between people who see each other primarily as a friend are more positive and fruitful than conversations between people who use the term "adversary" to identify one another.

When we are in touch with our friends, we realize two amazing things about them. They love us no matter what. They tell us to our face when we mess up. We are amazed that they love us regardless of what we said or did. We may not communicate with them for extended periods of time. We may develop a political viewpoint and loyalty markedly different from those of our friend. We may stop going to church, and begin to speak derogatorily about "Christians." Whatever we do or say, whatever identity we adopt, our friend remains steadfast and constant. We are touched by such enduring and faithful love.

Being in touch with our friends involves being held account-able by them. Friends hold us accountable because who we are, and how we conduct ourselves, matters to them. False or super-ficial friends are not invested in you enough to tell you when you have made a big mistake. A friend will tell you about your big mis-take, and what you need to do to make it right. This dimension of friendship is painful; yet it is redemptive and healing.

NEIGHBORS AND TOUCH

What is true about you is true about every other human on this planet. Every one of them was imagined, designed, then formed, by the Creator who deemed all of them individually as an innova-tive idea. That idea was shaped and knit in their mothers' wombs, and then at birth, they emerged as signs and symbols of the Holy Love that calls them into being. Their existence is a concrete sign of God's love for them, as is the case for you.

For your well-being, and for the well-being among our neigh-bors near and far, it is essential for us to stay in touch with the fact that we all are called into being by the Creator. We need to restore our touch with compassion, and our touch with the Golden Rule—"Do to others as you would have them do to you" (Luke 6:31 NRSV).

This past Halloween, a couple was on the verge of stepping onto their porch to refill their plastic pumpkin with a fresh load of candy. Before they could open the screen door, a small boy in a Dracula costume bounded onto their porch. He reached into the plastic pumpkin, and found it empty. From behind him, he could hear the sound of other children approaching. As the cou-ple watched, he reached into his own bag of candy, brought out a handful of candy, and thrust it into the couple's empty plastic pumpkin. They marveled at the compassion of such a young boy!

Our communities, and our nation, are losing touch with com-passion. Consequently, we are losing touch with our neighbor. A neighbor is another human being, a status or identity not limited to someone who lives in our neighborhood, apartment, subdivision, gated community, state, or nation. These close-by neighbors are important, and we need to be in touch with them. We attend to our neighbors in our cul-de-sac, apartment building, and other configurations of dwellings. We wave hello and goodbye, smile at them, stop, and talk over the fence or in the front yard, watch their homes and pets while they are on trips, and attend neighborhood socials where we can interact. These everyday, routine instances are the embodiment and enactment of the Golden Rule where people are treating others as they want to be treated.

Not long ago, high school coach Keanon Lowe came upon a student exiting a classroom. He was dressed in a long black over-coat, which only partially concealed the shotgun that the student had in his possession. Quickly, the coach disarmed the student, and then passed off the weapon to another faculty member standing close by. Then, the coach hugged the male student! The student melted into the coach's arms. When asked later by reporters what had prompted him to hug the student rather than throw him to the ground and restrain him, the coach replied that the hug seemed like the right thing to do. Maybe the coach saw a neighbor in need.

We know that we have neighbors across the nation, and around the world. These people are not personally known to us, but we know of their circumstances thanks to social media, the internet, and the news. When a natural disaster or a mass shooting occurs in another country or our own nation, our hearts are tugged.

When international disasters strike, be they acts of terrorism, war, flights of refugees, children dying of starvation, Ebola fatalities, an aircraft lost at sea, a tsunami, or mudslide, we experience empathy and compassion for those persons. We may pray for their well-being, or send donations to relief organizations. News channels and social media make these distant tragedies close and personal, pulling at our heart strings.

The current national and international experiences with coronavirus demonstrate the encircling circumference of who is our neighbor. Health care workers, administrators, politicians, patients, families, and medical laboratories around the world all are contending with this virus. Our hearts are tugged as we see news of passengers quarantined on cruise ships, people quarantined at military installations, and patients in hospital beds.

Strangers, immigrants, aliens, international citizens, foreign governments, and people who "are not like us," are our neighbors in fact and truth. They are neighbors because they are human beings. A neighbor is any one in need who turns his or her eyes to us, searching for a kind heart and a generous hand. The United States' Statue of Liberty is an icon of freedom and compassion, extending her hand to all who seek to come to our shores. She extends a welcoming touch to all.

These instances of our neighbor being the one in need point to the Golden Rule: "Do to others as you would have them do to you" (Luke 6:31 NRSV). We appear to be out of touch with this universal truth. The Golden Rule appears in some fashion in all the world's major religions, and has ancient roots sunk deeply in the past. Beyond religion, the Golden Rule in some form is adopted by the secular world, including atheists. It transcends categories and limits, as it speaks a profound truth.

To be in touch with our neighbors, near or far, is to show compassion. Compassion, or loving kindness, is the foundation for respect, dignity, and kindness being offered to one another. No one person, no one nation, no one people, no one race or gender, is superior to another. All humans share equally in the dignity of being a child of God, a creation of God, a being called forth in love. During this equality, there is distinctiveness and uniqueness, and no superiority, or "better than." Now is a momentous occasion for us to stay in touch with our mutuality, and enact the Golden Rule as we treat others as we want to be treated.

People living thousands of miles away in Indonesia were struck by a tsunami, which killed children, women, and men. A gas explosion in Russia collapsed a two-story apartment building, killing more than thirty occupants. Rescue efforts, after thirty-five hours, found and rescued an infant from the rubble. Who was not saddened at the deaths? How many shouted, "Yes!" when the news broke about the rescued baby? Recent fires in California obliterated an entire city, killed residents, and left thousands homeless. Who did not tremble with fear at the images of burning infernos, and the highway of flame through which people frantically raced to reach safety? The fires in Australia are destroying homes, cities, and are killing first responders, citizens, and wildlife. Who is untouched by the sight of the destruction, and the pictures of injured animals?

These news accounts all involve people unknown to us, and in three of the situations, people of a different nationality. One of the international events involves the foremost international adversary to the United States. Rare is the person who, learning of these tragedies, felt no sympathy or compassion for the victims.

Compassion disavows and discourages name-calling, labeling, blaming, profiling, indexing, stereotyping, and prejudice. Compassion speaks with the heart and from the heart, expressing solidarity with those in distress, and promptly sending aid and assistance to the innocent victims of a traumatic event.

With such behavior, we create and sustain touch with our neighbors by being respectful. Respect entails courtesy and manners. It demonstrates civility. Courtesy and civility shun name-calling, terms of derision, epitaphs of division, fiery rancor, hate inciting, mob stirring, and approval of violence.

Respect puts us in touch with one another. Respect is how we create and sustain touch with our neighbors. Respect builds bridges, not walls. People respond positively to respect, so that respect extended is the beginning of a relationship of reciprocal respect. Respect among and between people is founded on a common humanity, and on the universal Golden Rule.

COMMONALITY AND TOUCH

Now is the time for the world and our nation to be in touch with our commonality and mutuality as humans. Staying in touch with the bond of our common humanity is the proven antidote to movements of national and/or racial superiority. The Ku Klux Klan, skinheads, white extremists, Nazis, and nationalists can only thrive in a world of delusion and hate. Delusion and hate are the two forces powerful enough to freeze a human heart, and turn a human brain to mush. Such forces of prejudice, violence, and hate can be corralled by staying in touch with the Golden Rule. No one wants to be treated like a pariah, or denied their humanity.

We humans are more alike than different, a fact with which we need to restore touch. Our difference is that of 0.1% in our DNA. Restated, we are 99.9% alike! With a 0.1% DNA change of the requisite DNA ingredients, I could be you, or you could be me! How do you build "superiority" on the knowledge of our being 99.9% alike?

There are only four human blood types: A, B, AB, O. There is no fifth blood type representative of a superior human species. Science firmly and clearly demonstrates how we are quite alike. Hormonally, physiologically, anatomically, organ construction and function (including the brain), humans are all built the same way.

If you are a human, you have a four-chambered heart, two lungs, two kidneys, reproductive organs, a spinal cord, four extremities, and a brain with these eight major external regions: prefrontal lobe; frontal lobe; motor cortex; somatosensory cortex; temporal lobe; parietal lobe; occipital lobe; cerebellum. This medical science knowledge puts to rest any baseless claim for a superior human being. We are all cut from the same cloth. Let us stay in touch with some basic truths, and above all, in touch with our mutuality.

MOTHER EARTH AND TOUCH

We live in perhaps the most pivotal time in the history of the human species and our planet, a time in which our species is threatened with perilous blows pummeling our life-form's essential biosphere of oxygen, water, and temperature. It is a time when we have lost touch with the reality that we are stewards, not owners, of this biosphere we inhabit. Having lost touch with our identity, role, and purpose as stewards, we are the source of this threat to our species, and the planet itself.

It is a crisis of our own making because we have lost touch with our dependence on Mother Nature. We depend for existence on Mother Earth. Earth needs nothing from us, other than respect and humility. As stewards who are to tend to the earth's well-being, we instead have adopted the approach of taking what we want from earth, rather than receiving it. We rip up the earth, and take down mountains to mine coal. We take clean water and turn it into wastewater by cooling giant banks of computers, supplying manufacturing and chemical plants, and using drinking water to frack for shale oil. We fell the irreplaceable trees of the Amazon, then burn the trees, catapulting more carbon into the atmosphere. We are not honoring earth, or our role as stewards.

Our utter disrespect for the earth has us putting toxins into the very water we must have for hydration, and the very air we must have for oxygenation. As mammals, we have a narrow temperature range for sustaining human life, roughly between 40 and

95 degrees Fahrenheit, at 50% humidity. We are busy turning up the earth's temperature to life-harming levels—harmful to plants, animals, and humans.

Other species have become extinct, and we humans are not exempt from that fate. Ironically, the threat we face is not one naturally occurring such as the Ice Age, but one we have concocted and unleashed on ourselves.

The mandate to get in touch with our biosphere, Mother Earth, is a moral and ethical mandate, far removed from partisan politics. The counter argument to the moral and ethical argument is that of corporate profit. Greed is the basis for our potential un-doing. Those of the profit-driven approach are truly King Midas in modern attire. The profit-driven turn to gold whatever they touch, and in doing so, trade life for death—death of the air, water, land. We pump carbon into the atmosphere from smokestacks and automobile tail pipes for a pretty profit, and burn down the rain forests essential to our atmosphere, both death wielding actions. We pour pesticides, human and animal waste, chemicals, and heavy metals into our rivers, and pump dry our aquifers, while creating thousands of gallons of gray water from fracking, all toxic practices designed to make us extinct. It is imperative that we get in touch with what we are doing. Equally, we need to get in touch with what we must do to defend Mother Earth, and protect our species.

King Midas only came to his senses when he turned his daughter to gold. In distress, he realized that his gift of changing what he touched into gold just took his daughter. And, one might say, took away the continuation of his lineage through her chil-dren, his grandchildren. What King Midas learned is an urgently timely lesson for our day.

Now is the time, if it is not already too late, for humans to recover their humility in relation to nature. Being in touch with nature humbles us, for we see that we serve no purpose on the planet. We do not produce oxygen as do plants. We do not form coral reefs so than sea life may thrive. We cannot produce a food like honeybees do. Nothing depends on us. We are the dependent creatures. There is an old saying: "Don't bite the hand that feeds you." Humility is in order.

What we humans can do, and are doing, is alter the environment for weal or for woe. Thankfully, we have done things to make the planet more inhabitable. We have built dams, managed forests, and farmed our fields in ways that benefit and respect the environment. We have lowered carbon emissions, created biodegradable packaging, done away with freon, protected the ozone layer, and learned how to conserve and recycle water.

Because we have lost touch with the interconnectedness of all creation, we are introducing alterations into our sea-life chain of food. Plastic trash floats on our oceans, settles to the ocean floor, collects as debris on our coasts, kills birds and fish that ingest it, and is now showing up in human blood. The food chain affects all, including us. Our plastic, eaten by sea life and birds, makes its way through many channels to our dinner plates, and into our blood. A new lab blood workup may be our "plastic level." Air pollution and ocean heating are two other monumental examples of human power for woe.

What shall it be? Will we remain out of touch with our Mother, the one who feeds us? Or will we get back in touch with Mother Earth, and work cooperatively with her to restore this planet, and all its life-forms, to a state of well-being?

CLOSING

I author this book out of my sense of society's loss of touch, and from my personal awareness and experiences of being out of touch. People today are in pain given their lost touch with self, relationships, Mother Nature, and the Greatest Mystery. Touch ebbs and flows in a natural way, and this pulsing is not a cause for worry or fear. We can, and typically do, restore touch. There are, however, some challenges in life that knock us down, putting us out of touch for protracted periods of time.

This book attempts to address these more chronic and acute moments of lost touch. My purpose is to contribute to your efforts to restore the touch that means so much to you, others, and the planet. I suggest that you begin with your sense of the Greatest Mystery, and the realization of a reality that exists on the other side of the thin veil. I am convinced that restored touch across the fabric of life requires a spiritual awakening. Life is bigger than the small box into which we try to fit it.

BIBLIOGRAPHY

American Psychiatric Association. *Diagnostic and Statistical Manual of Mental Disorders: DSM-5*. Arlington, VA: APA, DSM-5 Task Force, 2013.

Atwell, Robert. *Celebrating the Seasons: Daily Spiritual Readings for the Christian Year*. Harrisburg, PA: Morehouse, 2001.

Bowen, Murray. *Family Therapy in Clinical Practice*. New York: Aronson, 1985.

Bowlby, John. *Attachment and Loss*. 2nd ed. 3 vols. New York: Basic, 1983.

Hertenstein, Matthew J., et al. "Touch Communicates Distinct Emotions." *Emotions* 6 (2006) 528–33.

Keltner, Dacher. *Born to Be Good :The Science of a Meaningful Life*. New York: Norton, 2009.

———. "Hands On Research: The Science of Touch." Article with accompanying YouTube video (7:54). *Greater Good*, September 29, 2010. https://greatergood.berkeley.edu/article/item/hands_on_research.

Minuchin, Salvador. *Families and Family Therapy*. Cambridge: Harvard University Press, 1979.

www.ingramcontent.com/pod-product-compliance
Lightning Source LLC
Chambersburg PA
CBHW071838090426
42737CB00012B/2293